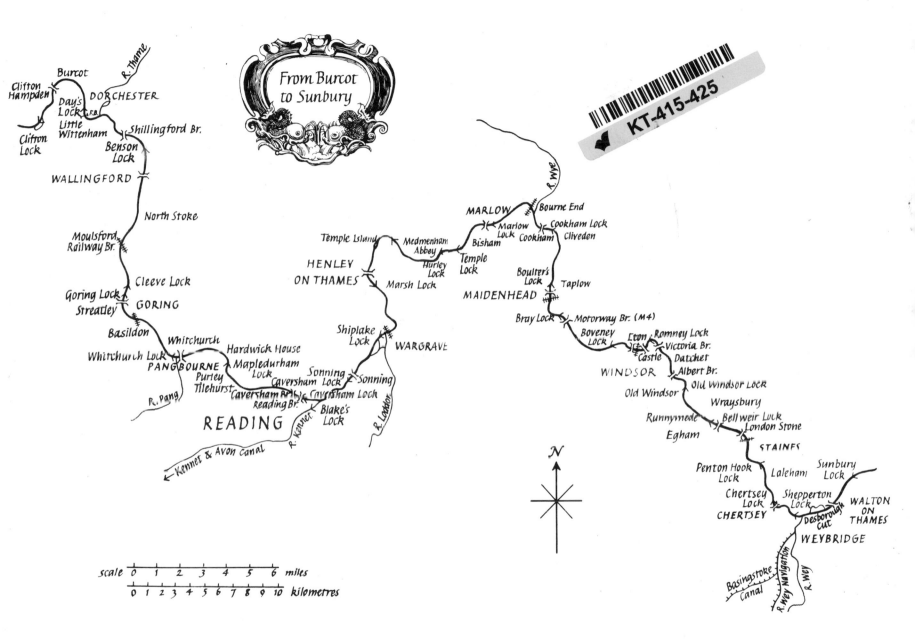

From Burcot to Sunbury

KT-415-425

Clifton Hampden
Burcot
Clifton Lock
Day's Lock
DORCHESTER
F.B.
Little Wittenham
Shillingford Br.
R. Thame
Benson Lock
WALLINGFORD
North Stoke
Moulsford Railway Br.
Cleeve Lock
Goring Lock
Streatley
GORING
Basildon
Whitchurch
Whitchurch Lock
Hardwick House
PANGBOURNE
Mapledurham Lock
Purley
Tilehurst
Caversham
R. Pang
Caversham Bridge
Reading Br.
Caversham Lock
Blake's Lock
READING
Kennet & Avon Canal
R. Kennet
R. Loddon
Sonning Lock
Sonning
Shiplake Lock
WARGRAVE
Temple Island
Medmenham Abbey
HENLEY ON THAMES
Hurley Lock
Marsh Lock
Temple Lock
Bisham
MARLOW
Marlow Lock
Bourne End
Cookham
Cookham Lock
Cliveden
R. Wye
Boulter's Lock
Taplow
MAIDENHEAD
Bray Lock
Motorway Br. (M4)
Boveney Lock
Eton
Castle
Romney Lock
Victoria Br.
Datchet
WINDSOR
Albert Br.
Old Windsor
Old Windsor Lock
Wraysbury
Runnymede
Egham
Bell weir Lock
London Stone
STAINES
Penton Hook Lock
Laleham
Sunbury Lock
Chertsey Lock
CHERTSEY
Shepperton Lock
Desborough Cut
WALTON ON THAMES
WEYBRIDGE
Basingstoke Canal
R. Wey Navigation
R. Wey

N

scale 0 1 2 3 4 5 6 miles
0 1 2 3 4 5 6 7 8 9 10 kilometres

A YEAR ON THE THAMES

*This book is dedicated to all who
appreciate the beauty of the River Thames
. . . in the hope that its beauty will always
be here to be appreciated.*

A YEAR ON THE THAMES

Paul Felix and Bill Charlton

ALAN SUTTON

First published in the United Kingdom in 1990 by
Alan Sutton Publishing Ltd · Phoenix Mill · Stroud · Gloucestershire

First published in the United States of America in 1990 by
Alan Sutton Publishing Inc · Wolfeboro Falls · NH 03896–0848

British Library Cataloguing in Publication Data

Felix, Paul, *1942–*
A year on the Thames
1. England. Thames River, history
I. Title   II. Charlton, Bill, *1932–*
942.2

ISBN 0–86299–738–0

Library of Congress Cataloguing in Publication Data applied for

Title Page Photograph: Pangbourne

Contents Page Photograph: Streatley

Typeset in 10/11pt Bembo
Typesetting and origination by
Alan Sutton Publishing Limited.
Colour Separation by Spa Graphics Limited, Cheltenham
Printed in Great Britain by
BPCC Paulton Books Limited

CONTENTS

I have seen the Mississippi,
That is muddy water.
I have seen the St Lawrence,
That is crystal water.
But the Thames is liquid history.

John Burns

INTRODUCTION

The River Thames has, through the years, served as a highway, line of defence, trade route, natural playground, sports arena and major tourist attraction. Despite its immense popularity, resulting in millions of visitors each year, it is still the ideal location to 'get away from it all'. But it is much more. It is one of the friendliest rivers in the world. Those living and working along its route seem to pulsate with their own particular brand of warmth and this is a contributing factor to the river's appeal.

People from all walks of life and of all ages and nationalities look upon the longest river wholly in England as a source of varied pleasure, especially those taking delight in one of our favourite national pastimes, 'messing around in boats'. Having lived and worked within yards of the river we have both learned to appreciate and to value its unique qualities.

For hundreds of years these qualities have been enjoyed by others, but the value of the Thames as a leisure area did not become fully appreciated until the expansion of the railways. Suddenly miles of unspoilt countryside were opened up to thousands of families and as pleasure seekers became more adventurous they penetrated deeper inland and boosted the popularity of such riverside havens as Windsor, Maidenhead, Marlow, Henley and Abingdon. Day trips developed into weekend breaks and week long holidays. It was not just the river itself which had appeal, but its adjacent towns, villages and hamlets. Today it is still possible to explore the route of the river at a leisurely pace, discovering acres of one of the most beautiful areas of England unfurling before your eyes.

In the early days of river exploration transport was provided by log rafts, crudely made boats cut out of tree trunks and hide-covered craft so small they could be carried on one's back. The volume of river craft gradually increased with new designs launched from the yards of some of the finest small-boat builders in the world.

Popularity brings its problems to such a beauty spot. One hundred years ago concern was being expressed about the damage being inflicted. In London the Thames was described as 'a river of floating filth', banks were being scarred and the lifelong habits of wildlife were being changed by so much increased activity. Steps have since been

LECHLADE
Houseboats marooned as the river floods its banks

taken to improve the general condition of the river. Even an ambitious project to reintroduce salmon to the waters is meeting a high degree of success.

Why the river is so popular is not hard to see. It is not only visually attractive but offers an amazing variety of facilities and amenities on land and water. Multi-million pound marinas, luxury hotels and restaurants, the small public houses offering ploughman's lunches – all contribute. Bank holidays and Summer months may see convoys of boats of all shapes and sizes steered with a variety of skills, but rarely is witnessed the impatience that boils over on motorways. You may have to queue at a busy lock, but tempers never fray as they do at snarled up interchanges. Lock-keepers display a calmness and friendship which is reflected along the entire river. It is one of the features of river life.

Another of its attractions is the tidy, orderly air which hangs over it. It could so easily become an eyesore of crisp packets, picnic rubbish, soft drink cans. Yet it is to the credit of those living within its reaches that such a problem never seems to get out of hand. It is also a credit to professional and amateur watchdogs that development has, in the main, failed to detract from the natural beauty of the Thames. Members of the River Thames Society, for example, scan every proposed planning application and its members are quick to voice their feelings if they feel their beloved river – our beloved river – is in danger.

Much of the appeal of the River Thames is that wherever you venture along its banks there are pages of history waiting to be turned. And vast stretches have remained unchanged for centuries. Even within one hundred yards of London's Tower Bridge, in the heart of the dockland, you will find areas which look just as they did at the turn of the century.

Although the river forms the spine of the capital it is its little known areas streaming past lush pastureland that provide some of its greatest pleasures. It serves as the country's greatest tourist attraction, originating from no single indisputable source, but born of several springs whose activities reflect the varying levels of the water table from one season to another. It is up to us all to ensure that such a stretch of water which reflects the history of England remains a continual source of pleasure for future generations.

Paul Felix and Bill Charlton
Gloucestershire, July 1990

HAMPTON

Spring: A May day on the river bank as the blossom comes out and the Thames comes to life

SPRING

In the Spring a livelier iris changes on the
burnish'd dove;
In the Spring a young man's fancy lightly turns to
thoughts of love.

Tennyson

Although the Spring equinox on 21 March is traditionally regarded as the first day of Spring, it is not usually until the following month that this season comes into its own along the River Thames. It is a time of westerly winds, April showers, strengthening sun, changing cloud patterns. When many water plants spurt into growth, when the cuckoo makes its classic call, when snipe begin their odd courtship, climbing and diving with outer tail feathers extended and vibrating in a curious drumming sound in the slipstream. When the warmer water sees minnows thriving in shoals in the shallows. When the stickleback male stakes out his tunnel nest, common crowfoot sways in the currents, fritillary graces the meadows.

Spring releases new energy for everyone along the river. So while we see birds defending their territories and searching for new-born broods, freshly painted boats take to the water, sails go up in greater numbers, scullers become a familiar sight from dawn to dusk and ramblers pursue their hobby in increased ranks.

Spring is the time of the annual tussle between Oxford and Cambridge, a sporting spectacle which for a few minutes captures the imaginations of people worldwide. For thousands of others, however, the Thames is a source of delight and pleasure all through the year.

Old Father Thames on the river bank at St John's Lock, Lechlade, the first lock on the Thames, on an April day

The excitement of Spring sweeps along the entire length of the River Thames with an air of expectancy. It is as if someone has scribbled a reminder of the arrival of the new season on a piece of paper, placed it in a bottle, and then watched it bob down-river on its way to London bearing a message for the whole world to read. Suddenly there is a burst of activity around every bend.

Winter wraps are removed from craft of all shapes and sizes, from punts to pleasure cruisers; the final build-up for the Oxford and Cambridge Boat Race attracts mounting interest; new-born lambs gambol in riverside fields; birds begin their courtship with bursts of song and amorous chases; the marsh marigold announces that it has survived another winter. Lovers walk hand in hand along the tow-paths and even complete strangers have time to nod a greeting to each other.

Humans and wildlife are creatures of habit, so in all probability you will see them returning to the same stretch of river as they visited at the same time last year, which may recall particular happy memories. The rest of the year is for exploration, but in Spring you take the first opportunity to visit your favourite spot. It may be the area you feel is the most attractive, or the most tranquil.

For centuries writers, poets, artists and others have debated with pen and brush which stretch of the Thames deserves the honour of being acclaimed 'the most beautiful part of the river'. The arguments will continue. How *do* you judge beauty on a river . . . a family of swans, a deserted tranquil spot, a cluster of freshly painted yachts

A pale sun on the water – with once tall reeds – warms a March day on the river

with their sails billowing, the reflection of a traditional thatched house in the water?

In 1870 the writer Horace Walpole took one look at the river as it headed north for the last time past Nuneham Courtney and described it as 'the most beautiful place in the world'. An identical opinion was expressed some years earlier by the first Lord Harcourt. Which is why he went to the trouble of completely demolishing the village in order to build on the site one of the finest mansions in Oxfordshire! It so impressed Queen Victoria and Prince Albert that they spent their honeymoon

EYOT ISLAND, LONDON
Low water as the river starts its way through the capital on a cold April morning

LECHLADE
A May afternoon, as the trees come into leaf next to the boatyard, some 130 miles from the sea

Cotswold stone and Spring flowers on the bank of the
stripling river which makes its way through Ewen village

stump on the side of a hill can be found an old
wooden seat bearing testimony to this opposition:

> This tree was planted by one Babra Wyatt who
> was so attached to it that at the removal of the
> village of Nuneham Courtney she earnestly
> entreated that she might remain in her olde
> habitation. Her request was complied with and
> her cottage not pulled down till after her death.
> Anno 1760

there in 1840. Lord Harcourt rebuilt the village
along the Henley–Oxford road and secured the
services of architect Stiff Leadbetter to build 'an
enormous house in golden stone'. Capability
Brown was called in to lay out the grounds,
complete with temples, statues and follies. His
lordship's decision after he proclaimed 'the village
spoils my view' may seem rather drastic, but
moving the population to new homes certainly
improved their living standards. Hovels were
replaced by modern buildings, although moving
did not please everyone. Beneath an ivy covered

You cannot see the village from this part of the
river and, unfortunately, you cannot see the river
from the village. Nuneham Park is now owned by
Oxford University and serves as a conference
centre. All roads leading through the estate
towards the river are marked 'private'. For the
best view of this stretch which so impressed
Walpole you have to walk up the west bank from
Abingdon, some 4 miles away, or find the path
from the village of Radley.

Lord Harcourt exclaimed that his new home
was 'as advantageous and delicious as can be
desired, surrounded by hills that form an amphi-
theatre and at the foot of the river Thames'. It
must have been a particularly peaceful spot in his
day. It still is, although the stretch is popularly
known as Radley College River, being used by
students from the public school. The college has
been here since 1874, founded in a Georgian
manor house which today remains as its nucleus.

There are many who regard the most beautiful
part of the river as that around Dorchester, where
tranquility has returned for the 1,000 inhabitants

NEWBRIDGE
A duck on the river bank watches as a canal boat comes through one of the pointed arches of the bridge on a Spring day

following the opening of a long awaited bypass. It is one of the most popular of the small towns on the Thames – and the most historic. It was here that Christianity in the south-west was founded by Birinus, a Benedictine monk who arrived in 635 and converted the King of Wessex, and established an abbey which took 400 years to construct. Birinus had been sent by Pope Honorius from Rome to convert the west Saxons and he baptised King Cynegils and his court in the Thame. The church the monk built here became the cathedral of Wessex.

For many years Dorchester has had strong links with the United States of America and tourists in their thousands make their way to this delightful area. The cloister garden is scattered with memorials donated by visitors from across the Atlantic: the lych gate was restored by Americans; trees have been planted in memory of President John F. Kennedy; there is another tree paying tribute to the men of the 7th Photographic Group who lost their lives in World War Two when based in the locality; a seat presented by the Women's Club of Dorchester, Massachusetts. The Great East Window was restored in memory of Sir Winston Churchill by American Friends of Dorchester Abbey and dedicated in 1966. The upkeep of such a majestic building is a continual financial headache. A £70,000 restoration project got under way in 1989.

Dorchester is probably the answer to most tourists' dreams, with a wealth of old beamed properties, some thatched, and ancient inns. There is even a stage-coach on permanent display outside

A blur on the surface of the river as the early morning mist turns into a fine day on the upper Thames

one High Street hotel. A path behind the sixteenth-century Fleur de Lys public house leads down to the Thames from the main road, passing a series of ditches known as Dyke Hills, which once protected the settlement of Dorcicon, a river bank town founded by the Romans.

Another area of great popularity is at Clifton Hampden, near Abingdon, where at the thatched Barley Mow public house, dating back to 1352, Jerome K. Jerome wrote a few chapters of *Three Men in a Boat*. The pub has often been described as 'the quaintest' on the river and the nearby bridge

Maidenhead: The fine bridge with its arches, one of the
many which cross the Thames along its length, bathing in a
pale May sun

Hills, is favoured by many as being the most beautiful. It is one of many historic sites along the Thames, for the Icknield Way crossed from here to Streatley, where there was a ferry for centuries before a bridge was built. Brunel brought his Great Western Railway line through Goring Gap and this boosted the popularity of the town around the turn of the century. An area towards Goring Heath has so many butterflies and interesting species of plants that it has been turned into a nature reserve.

Kenneth Grahame, creator of *The Wind in the Willows*, found Pangbourne, where the Pang stream joins the Thames, one of the loveliest parts of the river. Once an Edwardian leisure spot, there is now a toll bridge taking motorists across to Whitchurch. Grahame lived opposite the village church and died here in 1932. The book, published in 1908, was developed from stories he told his son and was based partly on his exploration along the Pang and Thames.

Tennyson frankly admitted that he was thrilled by the beauty of the river at Shiplake. He was married in the church here after a fourteen-year engagement and expressed his delight in these few lines:

> Vicar of this pleasant spot
> Where it was my chance to marry
> Happy, happy be your lot –
> You were he that knit the knot.

Sonning also claims it has the edge in the beauty stakes. The town was a Saxon bishopric before the

as one of the finest. It was built a century ago by Sir George Gilbert Scott prompted, so the story goes, by a conversation he had while dining in the area. His companion on that occasion was Lord Aldenham who complained that his servants were frequently missing the ferry from Long Wittenham. Sir George apparently broke off from his meal to design a bridge there and then – on his shirt cuff.

The 4-mile stretch between Goring and Whitchurch, where the river cuts through the Chiltern

the See was moved to Salisbury about the time of the Conquest. The river here is crossed by a 200-year-old bridge and features a lock which frequently wins the competition for the best kept.

Cliveden Reach, flanked by open meadowland on one side and the great cliff which gave the stretch its name on the other, has a strong claim to being the most beautiful section. So much so that it can get very crowded, with many seeking to glimpse Cliveden House, made famous by the Astor family and the 'Cliveden Set', and in more recent years by the Profumo scandal; it is now owned by the National Trust and is a luxury hotel.

Artist Stanley Spencer had little doubt as to the finest part of the river. It was Cookham where he was born, one of eleven children of a local builder. He saw in his native village 'Jerusalem in England's green and pleasant land . . . where the river is radiant and serene as the Jordan'. Spencer loved Cookham with an immense passion that he constantly strived to transfer to canvas; the village, its river, adjoining fields of wild flowers and even the local residents were all subjects he painted. Frequently he could be seen, especially in Springtime, exploring the banks seeking fresh sites where he could settle down to paint, and pushing his easel and equipment around in a battered old pram (still to be seen in the Stanley Spencer Gallery in Cookham High Street).

The artist did not like leaving Cookham for even the briefest periods. After attending Windsor School of Art he went to the Slade School in London, but always ensured that he caught a train

On a weekend towards the end of May the afternoon cools into early evening at Marlow, but still the river is busy

back every day in time for tea. He was working on a painting depicting the annual swan-upping ceremony when war broke out. Among some of his highly acclaimed works are 'View from Cookham Bridge', 'Separating Fighting Swans', 'Bellrope Meadow' and 'Magnolia at the Odney Club' – all painted locally.

To many, the stretch between Wargrave and Marsh Lock, the last lock before Henley, with its steep hills and woods, is one of the most spectacular. A mile downstream and you are in the town most identified with the river: Henley. Its noble

working water mill on the river.

Everyone has their own idea of what constitutes the particular beauty of the River Thames. Many years ago I met a tramp on the Chelsea Embankment in London who was convinced that there was no lovelier sight than moonlight playing on the water at Westminster. For me, there is a particular appeal about the stretch from Marlow to Bisham. Here the lovely old church fronts the river and there stands the imposing Bisham Abbey, once owned by the Knights Templars, and now run by the Sports Council as a National Sports Centre.

April time, a mother duck and her sleepy family sit on the river bank

Many will continue to discuss the merits of individual locations, but a stretch without much beauty, measuring just 4 miles 374 yards, attracts the undivided attention of millions around the world for a little over 17 minutes each year. March is the date of the Oxford and Cambridge Boat Race. Held between Putney and Mortlake, it is one of the most exciting sporting events of all time and can be traced back to 1829. The first race was far from London, though, being over a course between Hambleden Lock and Henley Bridge. It all began when a Mr Snow of St John's College, Cambridge, was persuaded to write to a Mr Staniforth, of Christ Church, Oxford, suggesting a match during the Easter holidays. Rowing at Oxford did not start until the Summer term, however, so the suggested date had to be put back. The course selected covered $2\frac{1}{4}$ miles, and Oxford won by several

five-arched bridge with sculptured heads of Father Thames and Isis, the sixteenth-century tower of one of the largest churches in Oxfordshire, the cluster of waterside properties, the backdrop of Chiltern beechwoods and the centre-of-river Georgian folly designed by Wyatt, make it a truly memorable setting.

Another stretch of great charm is where the Thames loops away from the outskirts of Reading and heads for the village of Mapledurham, dominated by the Elizabethan mansion built there in the late sixteenth century and with the only remaining

WINDSOR
An early holiday, as a boat makes its way along the river below the castle to the lock at Windsor on a late May day

lengths in an eight measuring just over 45 ft. Various challenges followed from time to time, but another race was not arranged until 1836 when the course ran from Westminster to Putney Bridge over 5¾ miles, a distance used by professionals for championships. Oxford wore white jerseys with dark blue stripes. Just before the race a piece of pale blue Eton ribbon was attached to the bow of the Cambridge boat for good luck. It apparently worked, for Cambridge won with ease. From then on the university adopted light blue as its colours.

Through the years the eights changed in appearance. In 1856 a lighter, faster keel-less boat was introduced; in 1873 a sliding seat was unveiled, something regarded as revolutionary. It was invented by a member of Nassau Boat Club, New York, so the American involvement in the annual contest goes back further than many realize and is not restricted to crew members. Gradually boats became narrower and longer to an overall length of 66 ft. Apart from the intervention of the two world wars, the Boat Race has been an annual clash since 1856. Race record for the Putney–Mortlake course is 16 minutes 45 seconds by Oxford on 16 March 1984, an average speed of 24.28 kph (15.09 mph).

Another spectacular rowing event is the Head of the River, a processional race for eights, instituted in 1926. Entry is limited to 420 crews (3,780 competitors). Also popular are the 'bumping races' at Iffley, where Oxford University colleges row. Crews race in groups of a dozen boats and the idea is to 'bump' the one in front and so replace

Cambridge and Oxford do battle as thousands pack the tow-paths to watch this very British event

that craft in position. The races, held over a four day period and featuring both men and women, are to determine the Head of the River.

Many of the sporting events seen on the river last a few minutes, others considerably longer. In May 1988, Malcolm Knight, Simon Leifer and Kevin Thomas rowed the navigable length of the Thames (299. 14 km or 185.68 miles) from Lechlade Bridge to Southend Pier in 39 hours 27 minutes 12 seconds in a skiff.

In March the toughest canoe race in the world takes place, when more than six hundred paddlers

PUTNEY
The annual battle between the light and dark blues on a March day is the first of many sporting activities along the river

ETON
The magnificent chapel of the College dwarfs the other buildings near the river bank. During May the Eton boys plan their boating activities

John Cox working on a new punt at Eton College Boatyard.
After many weeks of skilled work, May will see the
launching of this fine boat

need to time their start so that they arrive at Teddington to gain the full benefit from the ebb tide. The course includes seventy-one portages which can be up to three-quarters of a mile long. These necessitate taking the boats out of the water and carrying them around the locks or other obstructions without assistance. The race is open to any crew between the ages of fifteen and nineteen in the junior class and to those over eighteen in both the senior doubles and singles categories. There are no restrictions on the type of canoe or kayak used.

Many people are under the impression that the annual Oxford and Cambridge Boat Race is the oldest sporting event on the river. But this honour is held by the Doggett Coat and Badge, which is also regarded as the most ancient regular sporting event in the world, having been started in 1716.

There were many more sporting events on the river then than can be enjoyed today. Groups of river folk, in the main fishermen and watermen, had their own rowing clubs and met for lively programmes of activity which not only tested rowing skills. A strong element of fun was involved. Mop battles, or water jousting, took place with competitors standing in punts. Walking the greasy pole was a popular feature of a host of regattas, the poles being strung across the river to give added enjoyment to spectators. One variation of this contest was to place a pig in a box on the end of the pole. The animal was released by the first person to master the pole and then a free-for-all pig hunt ensued in the river. As the animal was usually also greased this was an event which could

embark on a 125-mile journey from Wiltshire, ending under the shadow of Big Ben at Westminster. The Devizes–Westminster Canoe Race is regarded as 'the canoist's Everest'. The strongest will strive to complete the course in under 24 hours; others are happy to finish in three days. The race has been held for more than forty years and follows the Kennet and Avon Canal for 54 miles from Devizes to Reading and then continues a further 71 miles down the Thames. The final 17 miles is on tidal water and competitors

BUSCOT
A canal boat makes its way on the upper Thames on an April day, leaving the lock behind

take quite a time and how many pigs actually survived the ordeal is not on record. Another idea was to place a leg of mutton on the end of the pole.

The sporting events organized by the river folk featured a variety of craft, even Welsh coracles. Dongola racing was also popular, with crews of six paddling punts. There was also tug-of-war in boats, usually punts.

There is a much more serious side to using punts in aquatic sport, however. A Thames Punting Club was formed in 1886 at Sunbury by a group of enthusiasts who ran Amateur Punting Championships. The organization was always struggling for funds and at one time it looked as though the idea would be short-lived, but in 1890 it was reorganized under the chairmanship of William Grenfell – later to become Lord Desborough – a man not only with considerable skills as an oarsman but also with a deep love of the Thames. Within a year his committee had organized the first Thames Punting Club Regatta on a course below Sunbury Lock. Two years later it moved to Staines, then to Maidenhead, and then to Shepperton. Lord Desborough was the longest serving chairman of the Thames Conservancy, holding office for thirty-three years from 1904. He won the Amateur Punting Championship in three successive years from 1888; as an Oxford undergraduate he rowed in two boat races; he became the only man to compete at Henley for the Grand Challenge Cup while an MP; he sculled in a crew of three from Oxford to London in 22 hours; and in 1855 he rowed a conventional eight across the

The blossom on the river bank at Radcot, near the stone bridge which witnessed action in the Civil War

English Channel.

The earliest sailing craft on the Thames date from around 1830 with standard gigs, skiffs and dinghies equipped with a mast stepped into a hole cut in the bow thwart. A small lugsail would be hoisted from this mast. But modifications were being carried out all the time as the sport gained popularity and clubs were formed to meet the demand: Thames Sailing Club at Surbiton (1870); Thames Valley Sailing Club at Hampton (1876); Upper Thames Sailing Club at Bourne End, the Thames United Sailing Club at Egham (now the

Laleham Sailing Club), Tamesis at Oxford, Oxford University Sailing Club and Henley Sailing Club (1896).

Sailing was also one of the pursuits of members of the Royal Canoe Club which was formed in 1866, although they were happiest with their Canadian and kayak craft. The club was originally based at Kingston but later moved to Trowlock Island, Teddington.

Punts were also used for sailing and among those enjoying this sport was aircraft pioneer Thomas Sopwith. The sport probably reached its height of popularity about the turn of the century, the two most popular venues being Henley and Kingston Reach. Punts bore masts up to 19 ft, carrying 150 sq ft of canvas. Most masts and booms were of bamboo.

Canoe racing has always been popular, although in recent years a variation has been the 'slalom' events with courses laid out in testing weir streams. Hambleden Lock was the venue for the first organized slalom event in 1954 and others have since been held on a regular basis at Old Windsor and Shepperton.

The upsurge of river craft, in particular cruisers, has had a dramatic effect on the Thames as a source of pleasure for swimmers. Before World War Two swimming was extremely popular along the entire length of the river, to such an extent that communities had their own swimming instructors and official bathing spots, complete with changing facilities. Boats were banned in some of these areas. Once upon a time you could strip off and dive in as the mood took you, but Thames Conservancy decided to tighten up on this practice and regulated hours for bathing and drew up rules concerning dress.

Long distance swimming races were then a recognized sporting pastime and the Amateur Swimming Championships of Great Britain took place along the river until the 1870s when they were transferred to a permanent site on the Grand Junction Canal Reservoir at Hendon.

For many years a favourite occupation along the river, particularly among ramblers, has been to seek out the source of the Thames. It is an indication of the controversy surrounding the subject that one frequently finds explorers heading in opposite directions, each confident they are going the right way. There are two main locations claiming the honour: Trewsbury Mead at Ewen, near the village of Kemble on the outskirts of Cirencester, and Seven Springs, Coberley, which is also the head of the River Churn.

There are strong arguments to support either site, although the field at Ewen has long been known as Thames Head. But if the source is the highest point from where a river has its water then we must go into the valley of the upper Churn. An attempt has been made to clinch the dispute by erecting a plaque here. But there is another site which is worth considering. A little way south from here another stream comes into the river from the west. This can be traced to the grounds of Ullenwood House near Birdlip. Here, some maintain, is the true source of the great Thames.

BOURNE END
With the arrival of Spring the Upper Thames Sailing Club is busy, as all ages prepare to pit their wits against the elements

GLOUCESTERSHIRE
The source near Kemble; a March day – a small spring in a field is the start of a mighty river

Marsh marigolds after an April shower in once marshy land
on the border of Oxfordshire with Berkshire

It has been claimed through the years that all the streams and rivers in the northern area of the Cotswold Hills contribute to the Thames: the stream at the Thames Head; brooks flowing through the Ampneys and Maisey Hampton; the Coln which rises at Charlton Abbots; the Leach which starts from a spring above Northleach; the Windrush, formed by three streams to the north of Guiting Power and joined at Bourton-on-the-Water by the Dickler which flows down from north of Stow-on-the-Wold; the Evenlode, which runs from south of Moreton-in-the-Marsh.

There are those sufficiently intrigued by the subject to have spent years on intensive research. They battle on through controversy and confusion. The Saxon Aewylme Society, its membership made up of historians, topographers, students and other enthusiasts, has studied old documents and explored on foot. It firmly believes there is overwhelming evidence to show that Ewen field, where there is a multiplicity of springs and artesian wells, is the source. The site, as Yeoing Field, was recognized by King Athelstan in AD 931 in a Charter of Aewylme (Saxon for source of river or a large spring), which defined boundaries in a Grant of Lands to the Abbey of Malmesbury. In 1984 what was claimed to be a horestone, the original boundary marker, was found on the site by researchers.

Apparently the many springs and wells here all derive their outfalls from one immense underground reservoir. The water can be seen all the year round from a lane at the rear of the Wild Duck Inn. In times of extreme drought the spring runs underground and appears in a lake a few yards away.

John Leland wrote in the sixteenth century that the source of the river Isis (Thames) rose 3 miles from Cirencester, not far from the village of Kemble, ran through Lechlade and Cricklade and received the river Churn lower down.

The origin of the word Isis is also in dispute and many believe that it was originated by an Oxford scholar. The Thames has also gone under the name of *Tamisa*, *Tamesa*, *Tamesia*, *Tamesis* and, in Saxon, always *Temese*. First recorded reference to

GLOUCESTERSHIRE
Early light of a day in May as the river comes to life – soon the water will be busy

the Thames can be found in Julius Caeser's *De Bello Gallico* where it was called *Tamesis*, a Celtic word meaning dark water. Ancient writings saw the word 'churn' derived from the name '*coryn*' which signified top or summit and was applied to the river as the highest source of the Thames. Certainly it has never been known to run dry.

To add to the confusion, the figure of Old Father Thames stands at St John's Lock near Lechlade. However, it was moved here from the isolation of Trewsbury Meadow out of fear of vandalism. The stone statue was commissioned for the Crystal Palace exhibition to commemorate the centenary of Thames Conservancy in 1857 and is the work of sculptor Rafaetle Monti.

Lack of water close to the source means that the right of navigation on the Thames does not start until Cricklade. It is difficult to take a boat, other than one with a shallow draught, beyond this Wiltshire town. Early Spring is the best time to attempt it, when the river levels are likely to be higher and before weeds have grown. For the majority of boat visitors, however, the start and end of a Thames trip is at Lechlade, once a prosperous centre for barge trade.

Many disagree, but for some the Thames has no single indisputable or infallible source: the river is born of several springs whose activity reflects the varying levels of the water table from one season to another. Between the source and Teddington there are almost forty main tributaries feeding the Thames. Many are little more than peaceful rural backwaters, a haven for artists and countryside lovers. They pass through open countryside,

As the day starts, horses play in a field high over the river in the Thames Valley near Streatley

pierce villages, penetrate towns. All have a tale to tell.

The beautiful Windrush, so dramatic when it bursts its banks as it meanders through Gloucestershire and Oxfordshire, somewhat appropriately gave its name to Guiting, from the Anglo-Saxon *gute*, meaning 'flood'. The Cherwell, flowing through Oxford and a tourist attraction in its own right, reaches the river via Northamptonshire and Oxfordshire. The Lambourne rises in the Berkshire Downs, disappearing in certain stretches. The Kennet rises in Wiltshire in what was once the most

A stray rape plant adds colour to the river bank at Tadpole Bridge on a late March day. Soon the first visitors of the year will arrive

wolds gathers momentum to such an extent that the river can deliver 20 billion gallons a day across Teddington Lock in the rainy season.

Each Spring brings fresh indications of a growing public awareness of the many varied attractions offered by the River Thames. It has been estimated that annually there are more than two million regular leisure users taking advantage of Great Britain's 2,000 miles of canals and rivers. As well as those who gain pleasure directly from the water, in boating and fishing, others venture out on explorations by foot and on bicycles to visit the river and wander along its tow-paths. Making everyone fully aware that a river can be just as dangerous as a motorway is one of the tasks facing British Waterways.

In the coming years British Waterways plans to increase the numbers of leisure users substantially in all the various activities embracing the Thames, and it knows it will be necessary for newcomers to understand and appreciate the requirements of other users and to respect them.

It is to cope with this that it has had to introduce a Waterways Code. It is divided into three separate sections: Courtesy on the water; Courtesy on the tow-path; Matches, rallies and events. The first two point out to boaters and canoists, walkers, anglers and cyclists how they should act towards other users from their own particular standpoint, and the third has a twofold purpose. It has been designed to help organizers plan and run events in such a way that they keep inconvenience

densely populated part of England, and is joined by several streams and famous for its trout. The River Loddon joins the Thames at Wargrave, having made its journey from Hampshire. The Wey originates from the same county, collecting water from streams in Surrey en route. The Colne rises in Hertfordshire, joined by the waters of the Alderbourne, Bulbourne, Chess, Gade and Pinn. It fans out before joining the Thames, at several points including Wraysbury, Staines and Sunbury.

What starts as a trickle somewhere in the Cots-

SONNING
The fine bridge over the river in late Spring

to others to a minimum and to help other users recognize the value of these events and make allowances for occasional minor inconveniences to their own leisure activity.

The river must be treated with respect at all times. It must be remembered that it is usually deeper than the height of the average man and in many areas the edges drop away steeply. After heavy rain or following a thaw the Thames can run with considerable speed, particularly in the vicinity of weirs. An essential part of enjoying the river when afloat is to have good manners – and to obey certain rules.

Navigation on the river is contrary to the movement on the roads of Britain – you keep to the right hand bank. The best position to adopt is slightly to the right of centre, unless you are against a strong stream. Overtake on the left. This rule is the one which is most often either deliberately or unwittingly ignored. Upstream gives way to downstream. Generally, the cruiser helmsman must give way to everyone else as his craft is more mobile and easier to control than other boats; and a sailing boat cannot always go where it wants to!

All pleasure craft must be registered with Thames Water before being taken on the river. Certificates and registration expire on 31 December each year and charges depend on length and width. When registered, no craft may navigate the non-tidal Thames without a licence to do so. This is issued without further charge, but a registered owner must certify that the vessel is constructed and equipped in accordance with the Thames Launch Byelaws.

Goring: Boats still covered in their winter coats on a March day. Soon the holidaymakers will come and the quiet, sleepy backwater will erupt with activity

All mechanically propelled craft using the river at night must exhibit coloured and white lights: Red on the port (left) side, green on the starboard (right) and white ahead and astern.

Upon approaching a lock the keeper will indicate which side the vessel is to enter. He will usually be on hand to help with mooring and to give assistance with lines. These should be passed around a mooring bollard once and then returned to the vessel, one forward and one aft. They should not be made fast but must allow for the rise

MARLOW
On a Spring day the first stirrings of the holiday visitors are apparent on the river

On a late May day the bank is bathed in sun near the riverside town of Windsor with its famous royal residence

the higher level. The rate of flow of the river is underestimated by many and boats can actually be drawn towards these dangers. It is not uncommon to see a vessel pinned against the piles by force of the water and in flood conditions this can apply to bridges as well.

When approaching a lock you will see white posts in the river bed and you can moor against these in safety. Some have cross beams attached to assist with mooring. If the tops of the uprights are painted red or have red discs on them you must steer clear of them and not moor.

Keep an eye open for warning notices which are erected when the water level is likely to alter in certain conditions. These may indicate when it is considered unsafe to operate vessels. At this time all hire craft will be stopped, but it is up to the discretion of privately owned vessels to use their own judgements. All instructions must be obeyed at all times.

Permitted speed of craft on the river is officially 'a brisk walking pace', 4 knots or 4.5 mph. This is to keep wash to a minimum as it can cause damage to other vessels and to the river banks. Anyone who has been caught standing up in a punt as a large cruiser passes by can appreciate such a speed restriction. A 6-in wash can sink smaller craft and certainly causes considerable distress. It is advizable for all non-swimmers and children to wear life-jackets when travelling on the river – whatever the conditions.

Special care must be taken at bridges. Many have piers built into the river which form an obstruction to the normal smooth flow of the

or fall of the vessel, and be held by one member of the crew. The engine should be turned off – as should radios – in order to hear directions from the lock-keeper. Great caution should be shown when the lock gates are opened, as the initial flow of water, either filling or emptying the lock, is very powerful. The crew member holding the ropes has to hold the vessel in its position. If working the gates yourself in the absence of a keeper, always close them afterwards and leave the lock chamber at the lower level. You must keep well clear of weirs when entering a lock from

current. The increased stream which results as displaced water rushes into the arched spaces creating turmoil and eddies is a complication which must be foreseen.

The danger from the Thames was brought home in dramatic fashion in August 1989 when fifty-one party-goers died when the pleasure cruiser *Marchioness* sank after colliding with the dredger *Bowbelle* near Southwark Bridge. The Port of London Authority acted quickly and issued new rules to increase safety on the river in the area. All boats licensed to carry twelve or more passengers are now required to have VHF radio telephones which can make contact with the Port's navigational control centres at Woolwich and Gravesend. This also applies to tugs and other vessels 40 m or more in length or of 50 or more gross tons. Vessels 40 m long or more whose wheelhouses are situated aft, navigating upstream of the Thames flood barrier must have a forward look-out at all times in telephone communication with the wheelhouse. These ships must also carry one or more white lights of sufficient intensity to illuminate the bow so that it can be seen for at least 1 nautical mile in conditions of clear visability. Lights must be screened to avoid a glare impairing the vision of the look-out and they must not inconvenience other vessels and must not be mistaken for other navigational lights.

There are also rules for the vast contingent of anglers using the Thames. Fishing is the most popular participation sport in the UK, with around three million anglers a year applying for club licences. Many head for the Thames.

Youngsters get instructions on river safety on a May Day holiday at the activity centre at Longridge near Marlow

A rod licence is required to be carried by those of twelve years and over using a rod and line anywhere in the Thames Water region. Above Staines the fishing rights are privately owned and permission to fish must be sought from individual owners.

Thames Water also issues permits for fishing at certain weirs – including Bray, Boveney, Day's, Eynsham, Goring, Grafton, Marsh, Molesey, Old Windsor, Radcot, Romney, Rushey, Sandford, Shepperton, Shifford, Shiplake, Sunbury and Sutton.

TOWER BRIDGE
Surely one of the most famous landmarks – the Bridge with the Tower of London beside it – viewed from above on a Spring day

Except near tidal estuaries, rivers always flow in one direction. This constant flow of water is advantageous to aquatic animals which can gain oxygen and food from the continuously passing water with less difficulty than if they lived in a pond.

The riverside attracts many animals. Most are never seen. You might hear a soft plop as a water vole dives in, or see a small area of closely cropped bank and small piles of grass stems ready for eating and abandoned. If you see an otter you can consider yourself very lucky. Shy of humans in any case, they are rapidly disappearing from their traditional haunts. It is essential that we maintain undisturbed banks of river for otters to make their homes, and they also need long stretches of undisturbed water. Fish eaters, they normally hunt one stretch of water for a couple of nights before moving on. They use the river as we would a main road as they explore the countryside, and their territory will extend over many miles.

Otter sightings are rare. Areas of countryside where they were once frequent now report no sightings. In some areas otter holts have been set up along quiet river banks. You can occasionally detect an otter's habitat from its way of 'marking' its boundary with droppings, usually consisting of foul-smelling fish bones. Hunting otters is now illegal.

The Thames has always been a good place for ornithologists and its entire length teems with a vast variety of birds, although some species are diminishing. Details are given elsewhere about the welcome return of the mute swan, once threat-ened with almost total extinction on the Thames, but the numbers of kingfisher are giving cause for concern. This beautiful bird needs steep rat-proof banks in which to dig its nest tunnel. It is being poisoned by pesticides which are washed into the river and taken up by the fish on which the birds prey.

Herons are still a familiar sight, and cause havoc in small garden ponds in homes close to the river which they can clear of fish very rapidly. The mallard duck can be seen almost everywhere and is now almost tame. Too tame, perhaps, for so many people are over enthusiastic with the amount of bread they continually give these birds, round the year, that their natural eating habits – water and land snails, insects, plants, worms and slugs – are being ruined.

Canada geese too are returning in greater numbers, unfortunately not a welcome sight for farmers with land along the river as they can eat more grass in a day than sheep. Little grebes, moorhens and coots are still common; and in Gloucestershire you can see the curlew in river meadows and dippers in the adjoining streams. Kestrels have been sighted at many points, even in London. Fish are returning to the Lower Thames as it reverts to its purity of centuries ago.

The increasing volume of river traffic which gathers momentum with the start of Spring has however had a disastrous effect. Submerged vegetation has been shredded by pleasure boats and much wildlife has been scared away by the activity on the water and along the banks. There is still much to discover and admire, but some plants and

Today thousands visit Henry VIII's riverside palace of Hampton Court, viewed from the river on a May day. Henry would have travelled more romantically by royal barge

animals have either disappeared altogether from their traditional habitat or have become rare.

The need to conserve what is left is of paramount importance. Contrary to popular belief, however, such an awareness is nothing new. Concern was being expressed in 1884 that the popularity of the River Thames was having a serious effect on wildlife. The mounting number of pleasure craft was seen as a particular threat. A House of Commons Select Committee was asked to explore 'Acts for the preservation of the Thames and the steps which are necessary to secure the enjoyment of the river as a place of recreation'.

It was realized that steam launches were causing damage to banks and the profusion of water plants. By today's standards this damage was not great, but the launches were the forerunners of the fleets of motor cruisers which, while giving pleasure to thousands, have caused havoc. Plants which once carpeted certain stretches of the river and its banks can now only be found – if you are lucky or observant – fighting for existence in small areas of meadowland, on tiny islands, and in isolated backwaters.

Rivers naturally teem with all kinds of animal life and if they do not it shows we have been using the water insensitively. Treated sewage discharged into a river can do little harm providing there is enough water to dissipate it. But if the river is low the arrival of sewage will stimulate the growth of thick blankets of green algae slime that block out light and smother most of the existing animal and plant life. If the sewage treatment is not complete the bacteria continues to be active in the river, taking the oxygen needed by animals and plants.

Pollution can also have a disastrous effect on water plants. If water contains sewage or the run-off from a factory site or farm's heavily fertilized fields, it may appear to be clear of scum, but it could be that only fennel pondweed can cope with the contaminated water. A mass of pondweed can be an indication of pollution. Water contamination changes the entire pattern of river life, reducing the number of species seen – and in severe cases kills all forms of natural life.

River pollution is not only a problem near towns and cities. The combined effect of the increased abstraction of water from the river for domestic and industrial uses and nitrate fertilizers and slurry manure run-off from farm land means the upper reaches of the Thames are liable to great enrichment resulting in dense algae growth. If the river can purify itself all is not lost. The effects of pollution are watered down as it flows along and eventually, some distance downstream, normal life is resumed below surface. But there is a danger of one stretch of contaminated water linking with another to produce a continuous chain of lifeless water.

Plants generally have quite a struggle to survive in the Thames. Many are sliced by passing boats, which begin to operate in ever increasing numbers each Spring. Underwater leaves of river plants are usually ribbon shaped, swaying with the current and therefore offering less resistance. On the other hand, roots torn away by flash floods will quickly grow again and under some conditions will form dense patches which can adapt to the changing contours of the river bottom as silt is moved around.

The increased activity all along the Thames has led to much plantlife seeking refuge in backwaters. The Pang and Kennet have sheets of common water crowfoot; the Loddon has given its name to two rare and beautiful plants, a lily and a pondweed. The Loddon lily is also known in other areas, particularly Buckinghamshire, as the

Sonning: the early morning light with the pale sun of an April day, as the willow bursts into life

summer snowflake. It is illegal to pick it. Many other riverside plants are also protected, among them water figwort, willowherb, purple loosestrife, comfrey, ladies' smock, water mint, dewberry, meadowsweet and eelgrass. Protected or not, however, many plants are rapidly disappearing, among them the forget-me-not, orange balsam which originated from North America and the flowering rush. There are many boaters who do not approve of eelgrass being one of the protected species – it causes continual problems with propellers.

CLIFTON HAMPDEN
With Summer just around the corner the river and its banks are alive with visitors

Many plants which once flourished along the Thames are now few and far between. Himalayan balsam, however, a comparative newcomer, is spreading fast. It does well even in polluted stretches. An annual, its seeds take advantage of damp ground where dirty water has killed off other growth. It is also known as policeman's helmet, because of its distinctive shape.

Rich alluvial meadows can be found along the river between Streatley and Reading and near Cookham, and outstanding fields of fritillary can be found by the Upper Loddon and at Cricklade. North Meadow, Cricklade, is designated a National Nature Reserve and is largely owned by the Nature Conservancy Council. It is an ancient flood meadow of some 110 acres between the Thames and the Churn, and has achieved nation-wide renown as the best habitat for snakeshead fritillary (*Fritillaria melagris*) in the country. Hundreds of visitors make their way to this field every May. Here also picking is forbidden.

The continued existence of fritillaries is mainly due to the ancient system of land tenure still practised: the meadow is Lammas land – land where the common rights change on Lammas Day. From 12 August to 12 February commoners can graze their cattle and horses, but in Spring and Summer the hay crop is taken by the owners of the land. No artificial fertilizers are used and there is a large variety of plants and seeds in the pastures. The meadow is still managed through an ancient Court Leet which annually appoints a hayward to supervise the grazing and upkeep of the land and to collect fees due.

Tow-path vegetation is dominated by tall stands of great hairy willowherb, hemp agrimony and comfrey. Hosts of smaller plants grow on either side of the river, many hidden in the undergrowth. St John's wort, its history steeped in pagan festivals, and once used as a protective charm against evil, is still a familiar sight.

Brickwork acts as a good substitute rockface for crevice-loving plants, while crumbling cement provides ideal conditions for limestone specialists. Humid atmosphere above the water and in lock chambers encourages the growth of ferns, such as hart's tongue, and old wooden gates frequently become blanketed in mosses and liverworts. Old walls provide a home for black spleenwort and wall rue, while various lichens and ivy-leaved toadflax form a creeping mat over much of the surface. Hyssop is one of the rarer plants to be found in the backwaters and on canal bridges. Bankside herbs, such as the skull cap which has a history as a malaria remedy and cure for throat infections, are still used in homeopathy.

Many of the Thames-side plants are something of a puzzle, for no one can be sure how they came to the area. The Loddon lily, continually fighting for survival, is a perfect example. It is not a native of the River Loddon, as many believe. It originated in North America and it is not known how it came to flourish along the Thames. Many others assumed to be natives of the area are not: the sweet flag (*Acorus calamus*) originates from Asia; the willow and alder from China. The weeping willow (*Salix babylonica*) was first planted at Twickenham in 1730.

EATON HASTINGS
As May becomes June, this quiet backwater is ready for the Summer away from the busy tourist scene

The sun warms a quiet spot in a busy boatyard, where modern and traditional boats are made ready for Summer

Plant lovers would do well to visit the Chelsea Physic Garden, the second oldest botanical garden in the country, being founded in 1673. It covers 4 acres and has 5,000 rare and unusual plants. Another interesting location close to the river is the William Curtis Ecological Park opposite the Tower of London. It is the modern equivalent of the old physic garden. On a former lorry park, which may be redeveloped, can be found young woodland, a pond dug by volunteers and a rubble-based grassland which is tramped over by schoolchildren.

One of the delights of exploring the Thames is to note its regional differences and the way riverside dwellers have adapted varying techniques to take full advantage of the unique settings in which they live. The Thames may not offer such a dramatic landscape as other parts of the country, but it does feature immense scenic variety, a blend of both natural and human endeavours. The route is one of great interest for the natural historian, for each county is alive with its own plants and animals.

PANGBOURNE
A holiday boat makes its way early on a Summer's day towards the lock. Soon others will awake and join it

SUMMER

One may not doubt that, somehow, good
Shall come of water and mud;
And, sure, the reverent eye must see
A purpose in liquidity.

Rupert Brooke

Summer days are longer, the scents stronger. It is the time of the dog rose, wild thyme, cygnets and dragonflies. Foliage is greener, birds constantly clammer for food as they arrive in greater numbers. It is when a roar of combine harvesters in fields adjacent to the river mixes with the noise of holiday-makers celebrating their freedom, and convoys of motor cruisers seek quiet stretches. It is the time when rooks cry loudly to warn of approaching rain. When people who are not normally superstitious view the dawning of 15 July – St Swithin's Day – with some apprehension.

As humans change their dress as a mark of respect for Summer, so the mallard, the most familiar of wild birds on the river, changes its plummage. Chicks grow as big as their parents. Canada geese honk their disapproval at being disturbed. The kingfisher seeks a rat-proof nest, while coots squabble over territories established among reeds. Midges swarm over the water, the horsefly carries out its silent attack, water spiders strut across the surface of the river.

Riverside homes burst into activity, caravan and camping sites fill up. It is time for Henley Regatta, that giant fashion show with oars. When those who have never been afloat don captain's cap and blazer. When the riverside pub becomes the centre of the universe.

A fisherman enjoys some quiet moments at his sport
before the boats are stirred into activity

The River Thames is a vast natural Summer playground which has for generations given pleasure to millions. But its popularity was given a considerable boost in 1889 when Jerome K. Jerome put pen to paper to describe a jovial romp by a trio of friends and a dog whose adventures took them on a voyage of discovery between Kingston and Oxford. *Three Men In A Boat* captured the public's imagination from the moment it was published (two million copies were sold within the author's lifetime) and drew their attention to the delights of a river holiday.

The book sparked off renewed awareness that the Thames could serve as a perfect location to 'get away from it all' and have fun. Pleasure craft which had enjoyed steady business for several years previously, suddenly found they were becoming crowded at weekends and demand gradually outstripped supply.

Expansion of the railways played a major part in tempting Londoners away from the city, offering them an enjoyable day out without spending too much money. For a few pence you could pack a picnic hamper and head into the countryside. Windsor and Maidenhead soon developed the air of holiday resorts and gradually the fun-seekers penetrated further upstream.

Many wealthy Victorians living in the capital, not content with enjoying the occasional day out, began to acquire fine riverside homes complete with boating sheds, tennis courts and croquet lawns. It was the start of the 'weekend cottage'. The properties bustled with activity over the weekends and during prolonged holidays and

Boats make their way through Shiplake lock on a sunny Summer's day

were either closed down the rest of the time or were kept open with a skeleton staff. The less well-off became tempted to buy smaller retreats.

For years the river had served as one of the main transport routes in the south of England, mainly due to the poor condition of its roads; commercial traffic had also built up. Now certain popular stretches became choked with holiday-makers as Londoners found they had a source of limitless pleasure right on their doorstep. You didn't need a map or a tourist leaflet to board a train taking you to Windsor, Maidenhead, Pangbourne or Goring.

HAMBLEDEN
A warm late July day, and the lock-keeper is busy as holidaymakers pass through

TEDDINGTON
The early, hazy light comes up over the weir and tow-path at the start of an August day

The late Summer flowers are admired by the many visitors to the famous lock at Bray

It is worth noting, however, that despite the claims that Jerome was largely responsible for boosting the popularity of the Thames, the *Universal Gazeteer*, published eighty-eight years earlier, had a special section devoted to holidays on the river.

Boats were not just something to spend a few happy hours on, however. As Water Rat exclaimed in *The Wind in the Willows*, 'There is nothing – absolutely nothing – half as much worth doing as simply messing about in boats. Simply messing . . .'. It was realized that the pleasure of hiring a boat for a couple of hours, or a day, could be extended. Sleeping on board and using a boat for a weekend's camping expedition became a happy extension to holiday planning. Campers loaded a variety of craft with equipment and slept under canvas wherever they felt like stopping, usually close to a riverside inn.

Owners of boatyards responded quickly to the craze. Craft were modified to provide canvas hoods. Soon some campers were setting out in canocs and when the weather was bad they reverted to the Red Indian custom of overturning the craft for instant shelter – day or night.

The popularity of the Thames was aided considerably by the foresight of boat builders who met the increasing demand for their services with a string of innovative ideas. When trains headed for the river in greater numbers a new form of boat hire was introduced – one way only. People set out along the river happy in the knowledge that whenever they became ted up with the adventure they could have their boat returned to the owner by rail for an extra charge of just 2/6d (12½p).

To meet the increasing demand for river travel the Thames and Isis Steamboat Company was formed in 1878 to ply a regular service between Kingston and Oxford in the summer months. The paddle steamer *Isis* covered the route and was such a success that within a year another had been added, appropriately called *Thames*. For three years thousands of passengers were carried until the company abruptly ceased operating.

By 1888 John Salter was operating the *Alaska*, built on the Thames at Bourne End in

Buckinghamshire, which left Oxford on a Monday morning, stopped overnight at a hotel in Henley, and reached Kingston in time for tea on Tuesday. The return trip took three days, stopping at Windsor and Reading. It was so successful, running over a five month period, that its departure time was linked to the arrival of trains carrying holiday-makers from London. Today the *Alaska* is being restored to something like its former glory, having been found on the canal at Oxford. The *Marlow*, built by Salter in 1902, can be found carrying passengers on Wilken Lake, Milton Keynes. Salter was so encouraged by the success of his first venture that he built a second steamer, *Oxford*, which came into service in 1889. Others followed at periodic intervals. The weekly trips were eventually doubled and by 1892 had become daily. Combined rail/steamer tickets became popular. By 1900 Salter was building his own steamers and over the next 31 years services were increased continuously.

Passenger traffic on the Thames increased with such speed that others began river trips. By this time the water was becoming so congested on certain days that lock delays made it impossible to stick rigidly to schedules and modifications had to be made to the types of services available. The craze developed by John Salter was built on by Joseph Mears Launches and Motors of Richmond, with a combination of charabancs and river craft. At one time the firm proudly boasted that it could convey holiday-makers to any part of the river, although it concentrated its main activities on the Richmond–Hampton–Windsor stretch. Even-

Hurley: On an August Bank Holiday the Thames-side locks are at their busiest, with boating visitors from all over the world

tually much of the fleet was absorbed into Thames Launches at Twickenham, now part of the Thames Passenger Services Federation.

Salter, however, continued to come up with new ideas. He developed 'holidays afloat' as something of a catch-phrase and arranged all manner of packages. If you had the inclination – and money – you could hire a steam launch complete with crew. The craft offered every amenity: fitted kitchen, toilets, even an engineer. With fuel and lock fees thrown in, a week's break before World War One

A warm day is just right for messing about in boats on the upper Thames at Wallingford

boatyards became aware that they were sitting on a previously untapped gold mine. Soon fleets of craft were setting out in convoy fashion.

New boats were built, old ones redesigned. Some that were destined for other waters were quickly transformed to river craft. Boats that had not been in commercial use for years were made into pleasure craft. It was not unusual to see a converted war-time hospital boat turned into a holiday home.

So many boatyards were getting involved in the holiday market that in 1955 the Thames Hire Cruiser Association was founded with the aim of coordinating all fleets and improving facilities.

Many Victorians and Edwardians had so much fun on the river that they decided to turn visits to the Thames into huge family gatherings, so domestic staff had to go along as well. Soon it became fashionable to travel in a houseboat to a regatta or other attraction, and elegant houseboats could be seen moored along several stretches of the river, gaily painted, covered with flags, complete with flower pots and boxes. Coloured lights and lanterns shone at night.

A large number became quite elaborate, depending on the financial position of the family. It was the 'in thing' to furnish them well and top London stores found they had a source of unexpected income. Some stores were commissioned to furnish houseboats from top to bottom: coal ranges were fitted in the kitchens, food was stocked for long holidays, ice bins were fitted, even wine cellars were installed, with regular supplies being sent upstream by special mess-

cost 15 guineas. At the turn of the century Salter had a variety of motor launches for hire for 4 guineas for two days. Comfort and luxury was the theme. Everything was done for you and you could venture anywhere, in any direction.

Salter's ideas caught on and were copied by others. Competition became intensely keen as more and more people found 'messing about' in boats could be fun. Those afloat for the first time were always made aware that staff were available to accommodate them – on condition that they were fed regularly. All along the Thames

SHIPLAKE
On a hot August day a cow takes a drink before picnickers find a spot for afternoon tea

engers. No cramped bunk beds for these craft, but luxury bedrooms, and verandas with comfortable chairs. Many houseboats were moored in isolated sites, others grouped together in unique floating communities. They became so popular that London-based businessmen would commute to their offices from their floating homes.

Competition became keen to establish the most luxurious houseboat. The title probably went to entertainer Fred Karno. In 1912 he certainly built what was, up to then, the most expensive. He brought in some of his own skilled work force to join local craftsmen and drew up the design himself. He wanted a craft to advertize his reputation as a master showman, so he installed a dance floor, marbled bathroom and made it clear that 'no expenses were spared'. The finished product cost him around £20,000

Boatyards began to specialize in building houseboats of varying sizes. Some of the finest came from Tagg's Yard, Hampton, which had already built up quite a reputation as an exporter of small craft constructed by its skilled band of craftsmen. A few were so big that they could not pass through locks, and some were built in two sections so that they could be split to pass through them. Most were towed, in either direction, to a special event, private party or public festival. They became floating grandstands for regattas, many with double decks.

The idea caught on to such an extent that soon they were becoming round-the-year permanent homes. As the craze for houseboats grew, so did the demand for horses to tow them short dis-

Swans busy themselves looking for food especially from passing visitors

tances, so another business boom was seen along the Thames. Owners of smaller boats jumped on to the bandwagon by offering themselves as specialist towers of houseboats.

Although the appeal of the river as a round-the-year home was strong many did not want to live on the water. The tranquility the stretch offered was a big draw – 'Getting away from it all' is no new feeling. So it was the turn of estate agents to benefit from the river's popularity. Hitherto unwanted parcels of riverside land were snapped up and wooden chalets built. Some fell down

TEDDINGTON
A flock of geese pass under the footbridge to the lock on a late August day

The fine, unspoilt view at Marsh Lock, on a warm August day, as the river makes its way towards Wargrave

along the Thames, regarded it as a natural step also to provide good homes for their boats. Some were enlarged for guests or staff accommodation, or just to become a pleasant spot in which to sit to look out over the water on a Summer's day. The golden age of the boathouse came to an end towards the end of the nineteenth century, but some of the original structures can still be seen today standing as a permanent memorial to a bygone era. Many provide an outstanding visual attraction, having been carefully restored. The majority, however, have disappeared. They were not always easy to build, frequently costly to maintain and susceptible to flood damage. It is rare to see a new one built these days.

Let us not float away with the idea that the Thames was first seen as a source of leisure delights with the introduction of the pleasure steamers. The popularity of the river this way may have flourished in the early 1880s, but people were enjoying its attractions centuries earlier. Elizabeth I enjoyed nothing more than being rowed on the river and Henry VIII was one of the early 'commuters', preferring to travel from Windsor to London on the Thames rather than face a bumpy ride on terrible roads.

when abandoned in later years, but others were extended. Not having running water or electricity did not always seem to matter; invariably there was a water supply near at hand, oil lamps provided light, cooking was on oil stoves.

There was also an increasing interest in camping, and such was the popularity of this form of riverside pursuit that in 1889 a Thames Camping and Boating Association was formed at Walton Reach, Sunbury, with a properly run camp site.

Wealthy Victorians, having acquired property

H enley *is* the River Thames to many people: gracious houses, quaint public houses, unspoilt meadows, all help to make the 'capital of south Oxfordshire' the jewel in the river's crown. It is a delightful place to visit at any time of the year, but in the Summer months

HENLEY
A fine view from the parish church of the famous regatta held during July and seen by thousands

visitors swarm in by road and water. At times it is as difficult to find a mooring as it is to discover a parking space. But the effort is worthwhile.

There is a constant hustle-bustle here which gradually calms down when the holiday season is over. But for a period from the end of June to early July a remarkable transformation takes place. It is as though an informal Edwardian garden party has been brought to life. For it is then that the most eccentric rowing event in the world bursts into a frenzy of activity. Henley Regatta is Mecca for oarsmen and rowing enthusiasts: every oarsman, whatever his capabilities, sets his sights on competing here at least once. They come from around the world for the privilege of taking part – or just to watch.

Regatta is a Venetian word meaning 'a rowing match of gondolas'. It was a sport unknown in England until 1775 when such an event was held near Chelsea Bridge. It was such a success that another was staged on Walton Reach and the idea soon spread all along the Thames.

The Henley regatta has taken place annually since 1839 between one of the finest bridges on the river and Temple Island. This also served as the setting for the first University Boat Race in 1829. The townspeople had always realized that having the Thames on their doorstep was of great benefit, and this race brought home to them just how advantageous it was. Rowing events, it was obvious, attracted public attention and a great deal of money was spent while everyone enjoyed themselves. It seemed the best of both worlds. So a one-day regatta was held, consisting of just three

A social and sporting event, the regatta packs the tow-paths with many thousands, all hoping for fine weather

events. After this first regatta the townspeople felt that such an occasion on a regular basis could be of immense benefit to the town, in addition to being 'a source of amusement, and gratification to the neighbourhood and the public in general'. How right they were. It has been held every year since 1839, apart from a gap during the two world wars, gained royal status in 1851 when Prince Albert became patron, and is one of the highlights of the sporting calendar.

What began as a one day event of three races expanded to three days in 1886 and to four in

Some come to be seen, some even to see the sport at Henley, the most famous of the many Thames regattas

they have been going to Henley Regatta for years and have yet to see a race – such is the appeal of this unique spectacle. For while every oarsman wants to row here, it also appears that every fashion-conscious young person wants to join the 'parade'. Henley attracts those who do not know a cox from a stroke, but it doesn't seem to matter. Regatta fever spreads like wildfire, engulfing everyone. It is as much fun being spectators to the spectators as it is to watch the races.

It can be argued with some conviction that the Henley Regatta course is the most famous stretch of any river in the world. Trophies presented in the early years are still being competed for today. Oarsmen train all winter for Henley, while fashion designers spend an equal amount of time preparing for the great day. While crews deny themselves various indulgences so that they are in fighting trim, others apparently deny themselves in other respects in order to save for new wardrobes. It is a time for old friends, new friends, fleeting acquaintances, romances. A cross between a beer (or Pimms) festival and a sporting event of Olympian proportions.

It is the time to 'parade', to walk and keep on walking, up and down, around and around the streets, along the river, oblivious of the crews preparing for international prestige. Tradition has it that this mammoth fashion parade begins at the bridge. With so many attractive pubs en route there are not many who return to the starting point stone cold sober.

Henley has always enjoyed hectic river activity. Wharves once lined the banks and cargoes were

1906. The original course was from above Temple Island to the upstream side of the bridge. In 1886 a new course came into use, from the bottom of the island on the Buckinghamshire side to Poplar Point. It is one of the longest wide stretches of the Thames. Interest continued to grow – and with it the regatta. Eventually the peaceful river banks were covered by acres of tents and up to eighty houseboats provided unique vantage points. The traditional carnival atmosphere has never changed through the years and it is extremely doubtful it ever will. There are many who frankly admit that

transferred to packhorses to go overland to rejoin the river further upstream. This shortened the distance by several miles and avoided difficult navigational stretches. It was a time when the river was as busy as the roads are today. The river was the town's main artery to London, and a source of constant pleasure and commerce.

As the regatta gained popularity hoards of university students swarmed to the town with their young ladies and, before long, going to Henley for the event became the fashionable thing to do, especially when the railway branch line opened in 1857. It is still so. Whole families organize their holidays around the regatta – and not just those living away from the town. Several local residents and others in neighbouring villages have found it increasingly advantageous financially to rent out their homes to visitors during this period while they seek a more tranquil scene.

The international regatta courses with their six lanes, covering 2,000 m and with high-tech timing devices, have changed the modern rowing scene. But not in Henley. This regatta is very much a case of 'as you were'. Two lanes are used and verdicts are still officially recorded as easily, feet, length and canvases. Where else at an international rowing competition could there be a fear of competitors colliding with a punt moving out of position?

There is so much that puts Henley apart from other regattas. Some of its peculiarities may seem somewhat eccentric to the outside world. Strict regulations regarding dress are still observed in the enclosures. If the weather is particularly hot, men

A tranquil scene on the river bank near Henley lock on a beautiful Summer's day as time just slips by

are allowed to remove their jackets – but not their ties. Dress hemlines are not allowed above the knee.

Some aspects of the regatta were even more controversial. A most extraordinary restriction was observed for more than a century, calling for the omission of rowers with a background of 'manual labour'. This resulted in the banning of a young American, John Kelly, father of actress Grace Kelly, from taking part because he had once been a bricklayer's apprentice! However, in 1947 he proudly accompanied his son Jack to watch him win the Diamond Sculls.

Ever eager to be fed, the swans are in luck as a passing
boat provides lunch on a July day

River punts and skiffs are the order of the day for
Wargrave's regatta

There is no doubt that in those early days – and to some extent today as well – the popularity of Henley was brought about by its enormous variety of inns, as the town was regarded as an important stop on the coach route from London to Oxford. Many are owned by the local brewery which has not only provided the town with its own beer since the early nineteenth century but also given England its only pope, Nicholas Brakspear.

There is much more to Thames rowing than Henley. Numerous stretches holding small regattas were once a familiar scene during the Summer months. Watermen's regattas were particularly popular and well supported. They had little time to follow hobbies but when they did they automatically looked to the river. Before club regattas were being held the watermen raced with fishermen and even crews made up from the local constabulary. As the number of watermen declined so did the number of regattas, although a few are still held during special riverside fête days.

One which attracted enormous crowds – up to ten thousand – was held on the Thames at the

SHIPLAKE

August is the traditional time for the annual break, and what could be better than a holiday afloat?

WARGRAVE
In contrast to the formal atmosphere of Henley, this village regatta which takes place in August is a family affair

small riverside town of Lechlade, which for many boaters is as far as they can travel upstream. The town developed the regatta idea into a water carnival and it was held on every August Bank Holiday Monday from 1903 to 1935. Events were not restricted to rowing, however, as swimming played an important part and diving contests were held off Halfpenny Bridge. This aspect of the day's festivities became so popular that the West of England Swimming Diving Championships were held at Lechlade for a time.

Another regatta which has maintained its popularity over the years is at Marlow. The atmosphere here comes close to that experienced at Henley and also has a strong attraction to oarsmen from throughout the country and abroad. This stretch of the river is used extensively as a training ground for several oarsmen, including the Oxford University Boat Race crew.

One of the peculiarities of England, and a source of continual amazement to many overseas tourists, is that no two of the many thousands of public houses are the same. It can also be said that no two stories concerning an individual pub are the same, either. Certainly this is true all along the Thames where many tales are a heady brew of fact and fiction, concocted, no doubt, on the assumption that such a mixture is 'good for business'.

The character of many riverside pubs has changed dramatically in recent years, unfortunately, as a result of 'restoration', rebuilding and modernization projects. Many smaller properties have made way for restaurants and hotels; others have altered out of all recognition while remaining pubs. A modern interior often scars a shell going back to the seventeenth century and beyond.

On the other hand there are others that have taken full advantage of their original 'olde worlde' charm. Publicans love to adopt tags for their establishments to put them one step ahead of their rivals. Wander the route of the Thames and before long you have encountered 'the oldest', 'the most picturesque', 'the smallest', 'the best garden', and so on. Often the same claim is made about different pubs. Jerome K. Jerome found the thatched Barley Mow at Clifton Hampden which dates back to 1352 'the most quaint'. The writer was so impressed that he stayed on to write some of the chapters of *Three Men in a Boat*, finding the low beams and oak panelling giving the once-upon-a-time-like atmosphere. And that was more than a hundred years ago!

Commercial drinking establishments are recorded as early as 745 when the Archbishop of York decreed that priests were not to eat or drink at taverns. In the seventeenth century, in the age of the coach, there was a massive boom in pub trade and many pubs today lay claim to being 'a former coaching inn'. In the mid-eighteenth century five London breweries each produced 50,000 barrels, each barrel containing 36 gallons. Towards the end of the century six breweries were each producing 80,000 barrels annually. A century ago there were 12,000 home brew pubs in the country. By the start of World War One the

ASTON

After a morning on the river, what could be better than to stop and have lunch at a riverside pub on a Summer's day?

number was down to 1,400. In 1966 there were seven, eight years later this had dropped to four. But there has been a rise in the popularity of quality home-made brew in recent years and today the figure is over forty.

Many ancient traditions in the licensing trade are carried on along the Thames. Brakspear's of Henley is a sixth-generation family business with more than one hundred and twenty tied houses within a 10-mile radius of the river. Robert Brakspear began in 1779 by joining a firm of 'common brewers' (innkeepers with a skill for making beer) and within two years had become a partner. In 1803 he formed his own brewery and when he retired nine years later its output was 6,000 barrels a year. Robert was succeeded by William, and at that time the brewery owned nine pubs and held leases on several others. When William died it had eighty pubs in its ownership. His two sons took over, supervised the take-over of Grey's brewery in 1896, and saw the number of pubs rise even further – to 150.

In the 1960s, when brewery expansion and take-overs were at their peak, the family business came under threat. Brakspear's approached brewery giants Whitbread and arranged the sale of a substantial minority share and two directorships, and avoided dissolution. Today Brakspear's continues to use only malt and hops of premium grade and in original form and its own yeast, and still makes four traditional beers. One old custom still observed is the placing of a bunch of holly and another of mistletoe every Christmas on a roof eave in the yard. According to tradition, if the

Time to watch as the world passes by on an August afternoon at Shepperton, for two girls sitting on the river bank

cuttings hang securely throughout the year the firm will continue to prosper. They have never fallen.

Henley has a wealth of historic pubs, many of which do more trade during the regatta than many rural pubs achieve during a whole year. One of the most popular is the picturesque Angel on the Bridge, claimed to be the most photographed and painted pub along the entire Thames. Charles I stayed at the Red Lion on at least two occasions as did Emperor Alexander of Russia in 1814 when his carriage was pulled through the streets of the

MAIDENHEAD
This picturesque lock has been visited by many over the years since the town became the first on the riverside to attract visitors

The hire boats at East Molesey await their customers on a June day when the riverside trade is getting under way

town by an enthusiastic crowd who left the horses drinking in a trough outside the town hall. William of Orange was another visitor.

Ye Olde Bell, Henley, is 400 years old and is a blend of timbers and low ceilings. It was built with recycled ship's timbers, a common building material in the town. Some say the Bull is older, and at the Old White Hart hundreds used to watch bear baiting and cock fighting from the overhead hanging galleries.

Traditional pubs attract good tourist business and if they have an interesting yarn or two to relate so much the better. The riverside pubs of London have much more to offer the customer than a drink, something to eat and a fine view of the Thames. The Prospect of Whitby can claim with some justification to be the most famous. Situated at Wapping Wall, it is said to be the oldest of the Thames-side establishments. It was renamed in 1790 after a collier moored nearby and has a varied history. Connected with both smugglers and thieves, it was also where Turner and Whistler wined and dined and from where they painted river scenes; where Samuel Pepys popped in when he was Secretary to the Admiralty; and where the infamous Judge Jeffries called in for a meal and then, for his after-dinner 'entertainment', watched the public hangings of those brought before him earlier in the day.

The judge was also a regular at the Mayflower in Rotherhithe Street, originally known as the Shippe Inn. It was renamed in 1611 after the *Mayflower* moored nearby ready to sail with the Pilgrim Fathers to the New World – in fact it is said that the captain was standing at the bar enjoying a drink when he received his assignment for the trip. The jetty offers wonderful views of the Thames and is extensively used in summer. An unusual aspect of the pub is that it has a special post office licence which allows it to sell both English and American postage stamps. The building was severely damaged during the Blitz when it received a direct hit from a bomb, but was restored. It retains its original steel floodgates.

Yet another pub associated with Judge Jeffries is the Angel at Bermondsey Wall. There is even evidence that on occasions he held his court here. Other regulars included Samuel Pepys, Captain Cook, and Laurel and Hardy. There has been a tavern on the site since monks from Bermondsey Priory built one in the fifteenth century and there are fine views towards Tower Bridge in one direction and the Pool of London in the other. To many it offers the finest views of any pub in the area.

Charles Dickens is associated with many of these riverside pubs and gained material for his books while in the area. It is believed he created his six jolly fellowship porters for his novel *Our Mutual Friend* as a result of visits to The Grapes in Narrow Street in the heart of London's Dockland. The pub dates from the sixteenth century and has a long history associated with literary and dockland life. There is a Dickens Inn at St Katharine's Yacht Haven, Wapping, situated in a former eighteenth-century brewery warehouse, which was saved from demolition in the 1970s and reconstructed in the style of a galleried inn with much original timber and ironwork.

The Anchor in Park Street, London, has a patio looking across the river and this famous Southwark pub was visited by Dr Johnson, Oliver Goldsmith, Edmund Burke and actor David Garrick. The Globe Theatre stood nearby and also the notorious Clink prison which saw the origination of the term 'being thrown in clink'. The present building dates from 1750 when it was rebuilt on the site of a much earlier tavern, and it was restored in the 1960s. Samuel Pepys was a regular and it is said that from here he watched the Fire of

August Bank Holiday Monday, and hundreds are drawn like a magnet to the river bank to enjoy themselves

London to write his description of the blaze.

The Dove is a seventeenth-century pub in Upper Mall, Chiswick. Here James Thomson wrote *Rule Britannia* (a copy hangs on the wall) and while dying of fever upstairs also penned one of his lesser known works, *The Seasons*. The pub is tucked away in a Georgian alley upstream from Hammersmith Bridge and has what is probably the smallest bar in the country, measuring just 4 ft 2 in by 7 ft 10 in. Nell Gwynne was another who visited the local hostelries quite often if old tales are to be believed. One of her haunts was the

LECHLADE
Early morning on a July day and the fishermen here are already busy, like many more up and down the river

SWINFORD
Boats moored by holidaymakers after a busy day on the river

With the end of July, and the start of the Summer holidays,
youngsters at Eton are drawn to the Thames to fish for tiddlers

King's Head, a part fourteenth-century pub at
Shepperton which has been licensed for 300 years.

Oliver Cromwell used the Bull's Head, Strand-
on-the-Green as his headquarters; and the nearby
City Barge, originally built in 1484, was named
after the Lord Mayor of London's state barge
which was moored nearby. There has been an inn
on this site for more than 300 years and it has its
original iron door protection against floods.

Maintaining a strong nautical theme is a natural
for London riverside pubs. The Ship at Thames
Bank has a good excuse to display paddles, sculls,
river prints, rowing trophies and memorabilia
from the Boat Race. It is situated opposite the
race's finishing line. It dates back to Elizabethan
times.

The Trafalgar Tavern in Park Row, Greenwich,
has gone one better. The bar is arranged as the
forecastle of a sailing ship. Dating from the nineteenth century, the walls are hung with nautical
paintings and the river laps against the walls. The
Old Ship in Upper Mall is 400 years old and is
decorated with anchors, lanterns, sculls and a
model galleon. It is said to be the oldest pub along
this stretch of the Thames.

The George, Southwark, is owned by the
National Trust and is the only remaining original
galleried inn in London. It dates from 1598 but
was rebuilt – following the original plans closely –
after the great Southwark fire in 1675. It became
famous in the eighteenth and nineteenth centuries
as a coaching terminus. The pub was mentioned
by Dickens in *Little Dorrit* and it was here, in the
eighteenth century, that Lord Digby disguised
himself in shabby clothes to entertain, at Easter
and Christmas, thirty debtors he had released
from prison.

In Wharf Lane, Upper Thames Street, is the
Samuel Pepys, an accurate representation of a
seventeenth-century inn with extracts from the
famous *Diary* on the walls.

Many pubs still continue their old customs.
Perhaps the annual ceremony at the Black Boy,
Hurley is the most unusual. Here is staged the
Hurley Marrow Wassail, a ceremony originating
from a pagan festival to ensure good crops. A

RICHMOND
A red London bus takes visitors to the capital over the Thames bridge

marrow queen and her consort are chosen and also taking part is the largest marrow grown in the village during the Summer. There is a 'sacrifice' of the tree bird, with customers attending a burial service, singing and carrying lighted candles. Branches of the tree are dipped in cider and ale is poured over the roots. Morris Men lead a procession and return to the pub demanding refreshments.

As with so many pubs, the origin of the name is disputed. There is a local legend that the Black Boy was Charles II, after the nickname given to him in his youth by his mother because of his swarthy complexion. His complexion probably was dark, for his mother was part-French, part-Italian, and Charles was said to have inherited the looks of his grandmother, Marie de Medici. A more likely explanation for the name, however, can be traced to when Charles was trying to escape to France after the battle of Worcester. He was helped by a family who dressed him as a woodman, darkened his face with soot, and then hid him for a day and a night in a huge oak tree. This is a tale Charles himself dictated to Pepys in 1680, after his return to power.

The marrow wassail may be a unique ceremony along the Thames, but in Oxford we find an equally unusual pub tradition which has been maintained for years. The Bear, which dates from 1242 and is the oldest drinking house in the city, has a collection of around 7,000 ties, or pieces of tie, decorating the walls. Such items are only taken with the owner's consent and ceremoniously removed by a large pair of scissors. The donator

On a bright, warm Summer's morning a swan passes time gliding along below the once infamous old gaol at Abingdon

receives a drink 'on the house' for adding to the collection. Oxford has a vast collection of interesting pubs. Turf Tavern was owned by Merton College who sold the lease to a brewery. It was described by Hardy in *Jude the Obscure*.

There are many 'Swans' along the river, of course. That at Radcot stands near the oldest bridge (1174) on the Thames and is one of the river's most popular tourist spots. There has been an inn here ever since the bridge was built. Another famous Swan is at Staines; another at Streatley with a restored Oxford college state

OLD WINDSOR
A fine August day for a fisherman

On a warm Summer's day what else is there to do but to fish and enjoy the peace of the river?

barge tied to the bank acting as a bar.

Many riverside pubs have names you probably will not find anywhere else in the country. The Bells of Ouzely, Runnymede, is a perfect example. It stands where the original pub was bombed and gets its name, so the story goes, from the time when six bells were rescued from Ouzely Abbey when it was dissolved by Henry VIII. Monks took the bells down river by barge but at Old Windsor, to avoid capture, they threw them in the river and fled. When they returned the bells could not be found and have never been seen again. It is something of a mystery story: where was Ouzely Abbey? Its records seem to have disappeared along with the bells.

Another unusual name is the Beetle and Wedge, Moulsford, named after the tools of a woodcutter. The Rose Revived, Newbridge, was once called the Rose, and also the Fair on account of a horse fair held in a nearby meadow. At Cookham is the Bel and Dragon, established in 1417 and one of the oldest licences in England. Old Leatherne Bottel, Goring, has had a licence for 400 years and once had an ancient well which produced health-giving water.

Many conventional names can be found, however. The George, Wraysbury, dates from the seventeenth century and used to stage illegal boxing tournaments. Another George is at Dorchester, standing on the site of the original abbey hospice. It dates from 1450 and has its original galleries over the yard which leads to the travellers' lodge.

The Barley Mow is not the only pub to be associated with Jerome K. Jerome. Part of *Three Men In A Boat* was written when he stayed at the Two Brewers in Marlow. It dates from 1686 and the quiet road it stands in once led to an old wooden bridge, now replaced. Another pub with literary connections is the Trout, Godstow, which has served Oxford undergraduates for generations and was the guesthouse of an ancient nunnery. A regular customer was Lewis Carroll who first related his Alice stories, inventing the tale as he went along, on Summer boat trips from Oxford, much to the delight of his young passengers.

The Thames has one of the grandest and most stately of English country house hotels. Cliveden, the former home of the Astor family and standing in 375 acres on a bluff above the river, was opened as a hotel after a £3 million restoration scheme in 1986. Nancy, Lady Astor, gave the property to the National Trust some years earlier and the organization is still responsible for the upkeep of the fabric and gardens. The public is admitted to the grounds and on certain afternoons can also see some of the rooms.

Not far away, at Water Oakley, Windsor, stands another country house hotel of note, Oakley Court, with a 35-acre garden sweeping down to the river. When derelict it was used by Hammer Films for horror films, many featuring Dracula, and it also served as the setting for the *Rocky Horror Show*. It underwent a £5 million conversion before opening as a hotel. Built in 1859 by Sir Richard Hall-Saye, it is not hard to understand why it made such a perfect setting for horror films before its transformation, being styled as a Gothic chateau. During World War Two General Charles de Gaulle was a frequent visitor, which added fuel to the rumours that the property was the headquarters of the French Resistance. Hotel guests today can explore the river in a restored Edwardian river launch, the *Suzy Ann*.

One of the most spectacular events on the Thames is the annual swan upping ceremony to determine ownership of the majestic mute swans living on the river. At one

In the heat of an August day at Shiplake a fisherman is busy, with nothing to worry him but the size of his catch

time owning a swan was a privilege granted by the Crown and only given to nobility residing close to the river and to the City Livery Companies. Today there are three official owners: The Queen, The Vintners Company and The Dyers Company.

During the third week of July Mr John Turk of Cookham, the Royal Swan Keeper – a role established more than seven hundred years ago – sets out upriver to Henley, the upper limit of his jurisdiction, accompanied by swan keepers of the two companies. It is an occasion steeped in tradi-

The Queen's swanmaster, Fred Turk, prepares for the traditional swan-upping which dates from the sixteenth century

It is no easy task, for Mr Turk and his helpers are dealing with one of the heaviest flying birds in the world. The male, which has been known to show aggression towards man, usually weighs around 12 kg, but can reach 15 kg or 16 kg. Little wonder that at one time the main interest in swans was culinary.

The mute swan is the only swan living in Britain all the year round. Its origins have always been a matter of considerable conjecture. Now they are virtually wild but they originated from domestic or semi-domestic birds centuries ago. There is a tale that Richard the Lionheart introduced them from Cyprus; others believe they were brought to England from Europe; and there are those who are firmly convinced that they are an indigenous species.

In the 1950s swans were considered something of a nuisance on the Thames because of their large numbers. In 1956 a count revealed as many as 1,300 along the river, of which 200 were cygnets. In less than thirty years the position had changed dramatically, the number of adults being 200, with 32 cygnets. Fears were expressed that the swan, which for so many people conjures up a picture of the River Thames, might become extinct.

Although the vastly increased use of the river in recent years by pleasure seekers and major engineering works have been contributing factors to this sharp decline, the greatest danger came from anglers' lead weights. Swans are bottom feeders, taking up gravel to help them grind the fronds of water plants on which they feed. This put them at

tion and Mr Turk has been supervizing the delicate operation since 1963, when he took over from his father.

The Royal Swan Keeper uses a traditional Thames craft, a randan, while his assistants use double sculling skiffs. They carry long-handled crooks to catch the birds which are then marked for identification purposes. While Royal swans remain unmarked, the Vintners' swans have marks cut on either side of the mandible; the Dyers' swans have a single mark. If there is any bleeding it is stopped with the use of pitch.

SWAN-UPPING
The swan-uppers prepare to leave Marlow for the annual July count and marking of cygnets along the river

risk from lead weights and shotgun pellets which lie on the river bed. The lead is worn down in the gizzard and poisons the birds. Lead weights were found in the gizzards of swans and blood tests showed high lead levels.

A ban on the sale of certain lead weights by the 1987 Control of Pollution Act has since seen a dramatic recovery in the mute swan population. Shortly after the introduction of the Act ten water authorities in England and Wales brought in bye-laws banning the use of lead weights for fishing between 0.06 g and 8.36 g. There was a marked response from anglers. Monitoring of the position has continued and it has been found that the number of swans found dead or rescued with lead poisoning has almost halved and there has been a marked reduction in the amount of lead found in live swans. As a result, the mute swan population on the Thames, has increased by 26 per cent.

Swans are appearing in greater numbers all the way along the river from London to Gloucestershire and on its tributaries. Marlow, Henley, Oxford and Abingdon in particular have all seen a big increase in their swan populations. This is because the chances of cygnets surviving has strengthened. In the early 1980s as many as 80 per cent of cygnets died within twelve months of hatching and only one in ten lived four years. There are also signs that swans are maturing at an earlier age. Mute swans are normally aged three or four when they first breed, but in recent years 12 of the 78 first time breeders on the Thames have been aged just two. This has all helped towards the rise in swan population along the river.

A team from Oxford University weighs swans as part of its research into lead and pollution poisoning

The dangers to swans are not restricted to lead poisoning, however. Work is going on to re-establish aquatic vegetation in rivers and to protect traditional nest sites. There is also an attempt being made to cut down on the number of swans who die as a result of colliding with power lines and electricity boards have been carrying out tests to see how this problem can be minimized.

Exactly how many mute swans there are today can only be guessed at, which is why in 1990 the Wildfowl and Wetlands Trust at Slimbridge launched a nationwide census. Hundreds of

COOKHAM
The end of a perfect Summer's day in late August

volunteers all over England, Scotland and Wales have been called in to help and, in conjunction with the British Trust for Ornithology, it is planned to build up a picture both of the total number of mute swans in Britain and their geo-graphical distribution. The result is awaited with interest, because in the early 1980s the Nature Conservancy Council produced the startling stat-istic that between 3,000 and 4,000 mute swans were dying every year.

CLIVEDEN REACH
Said by many to be the most beautiful spot on the Thames, it is seen here at its best on an autumnal September day

AUTUMN

No Spring, nor Summer beauty hath such grace,
As I have seen in one Autumnal face.

John Donne

Autumn can be one of the best times of the year for exploring the Thames and certainly it is at its loveliest as the river gradually changes colour. Once the crowds have gone a hushed calmness descends, apart from those occasions when the skies darken as thousands of birds gather for migration. Many of the smaller ones will meet as night falls, however, with the knowledge that darkness offers protection against predators. Cool clear nights bring out sweaters for protection of a different kind as frost brings down the bright ochre leaves off the beech trees.

Farmers prepare their soil as sparrows creep across the fields of stubble searching for spent grain, and the long tailed field mouse shows more activity than he has displayed all year as he hunts for supplies. Piles of old bracken and grass appear outside the sets of badgers as the sows clean out their chambers. The red admiral butterfly feeds on late flowering plants. Visiting quail rustle through the long grass.

It is a time when fair weather boaters pack up their craft for another year. There are many, however, who keep their wraps still tucked away, knowing only too well the attractions of meandering along the river during Autumn when lock delays are a thing of the past.

A picturesque cottage nestles on the river bank at
Cliveden Reach, as the trees behind climb vertically
to the stately home

WINDSOR
A pale November sun lights the bridge which leads from sleepy Eton High Street across to the castle

At one time the River Thames was so shallow in places that it was possible to cross from one side to the other without using either bridge or ferry. Julius Caesar is said to have waded across at Walton Reach and up to the end of the nineteenth century people were crossing on foot and by horse at numerous points along the entire route, especially during prolonged droughts. The Romans built their first bridge over the river in London 1,900 years ago and for centuries flimsy wooden structures carried traffic over the water. Many became notorious accident blackspots with travellers on foot, on horse and with carts frequently toppling over the edge. Most of these wooden bridges were either washed away by floods or else collapsed due to poor workmanship or extensive use, but many of today's crossings, which are such imposing features of the river, have been built either exactly on the site or within yards of where the original structures once stood or where ferries operated.

You will find bridges of Cotswold stone, iron and steel, and concrete. A large number are tourist attractions in their own right and in recent years millions of pounds have been spent on urgent restoration work to cope with the ever mounting volume of traffic. In the 1960s there was a serious threat to one of the river's finest bridges, the Marlow suspension bridge, which has provided a main link between Buckinghamshire and Berkshire since 1835. Possible closure and severe traffic restrictions posed a major threat to the prosperity of the town but fortunately a decision was made to carry out full repairs. There has been

The November light catches the swan, the emblem of Buckinghamshire, which decorates one of the medallions on the famous suspension bridge at Marlow

a bridge at Marlow since 1300. One of timber construction was partly destroyed in 1642 and a new one, funded by public subscription, was opened in 1798. The present bridge was designed by William Tierney Clark, a pupil of Telford. It has a span of 225 ft and is sometimes thought of as the prototype for the bridge across the Danube at Budapest which Clark also built.

London's oldest Thames bridge is at Richmond. It was designed by architect James Paine and opened in 1777, and though restored and later

A chilly day signals that Winter will soon be here and those who live on the river must keep warm

widened, it still retains its original charm. The oldest bridge still in use on the Thames predates this construction by 577 years, however. Radcot Bridge, built with Cotswold stone taken from Taynton Quarry near Burford, a dozen miles away, dates from 1200. There is a second bridge here, built in 1787, crossing a channel constructed that year to take planned extra barge traffic with the opening of the Thames–Severn Canal. Nearby is St John's Bridge at Lechlade, one of the oldest bridge sites on the Thames, originally built by a local prior in 1229. A toll was payable until the end of the eighteenth century. A later bridge (1884) carries the A417 Faringdon–Cirencester road. It is just below here that the River Leach joins from the left and the River Colne from the right.

Halfpenny Bridge, Lechlade, is the first 'real' bridge on the Thames, built in the 1790s and so called because a halfpenny was the price of the toll. It was built under an Act of Parliament passed in 1792 and it has been discovered that the footings for the abutments were laid on slender branches of willow. It now carries the A351 Swindon–Burford road. Another ancient bridge in the area is Newbridge, built only 25 years after Radcot.

One of the two remaining toll bridges on the Thames (the other is at Whitchurch, built near the end of the last century to establish a link with Pangbourne) and unique in offering its owner an unusual tax shelter, is at Swinford. Under the terms of the original Act of Parliament establishing its construction no taxes are payable in connection with the bridge or its toll income. The bridge was commissioned by George III after he had experienced a particularly bad ferry crossing. In 1764 John Wesley also reported that he was almost swept off the causeway while crossing by horseback due to the amount of water and the strength of current.

The history of this crossing goes back several centuries. A ferry here was originally owned by two of the large Benedictine abbeys in the area in the late thirteenth century. Upon their dissolution the vicar of Cumnor asserted his parish rights over the river and the entitlement to receive an income from it. From 1680 the leasehold of the bridge was

OXFORD
A quiet backwater near Donnington Bridge on an October day, now peaceful after the bustle of the holiday season

WINDSOR
The royal swans congregate under the gaze of the most royal of castles late on an October morning

owned by ferryman Timothy Hart and it continued in his family until the Earl of Abingdon acquired the ferry and land on either side of the river in 1765 for approximately £10,000. The present bridge was built for the fourth Earl of Abingdon under an Act of Parliament in 1769 and opened for traffic two years later. The Act stated toll charges of 1*d* per wheel for wheeled vehicles; 1*d* for cattle, calves, swine and sheep; ¼*d* for lambs; 1*d* for horses and ½*d* for foot passengers.

Ownership of the bridge remained within the Earl of Abingdon's family until the late 1960s and the death of the Countess of Abingdon, when it was sold privately. It was sold again in the 1980s when offers were invited in the region of £275,000. Today income tax is still not payable on the tolls received, estimated at 35,000–40,000 wheels crossing the bridge weekly.

Northmoor Bridge is another ancient structure, having been built more than five hundred years ago and still busy with traffic on the Witney Abingdon route. Matthew Arnold wrote *Crossing the stripling Thames by Bablockhythe* while travelling on the old ferry at this point.

Folly Bridge, Oxford saw fleets of steamers making their way to and from Hampton Court and is the home of Salter's Steamers. It used to be called Grauntpoint Bridge but was renamed in the seventeenth century after a folly built at one end. For a time it was an accident blackspot because it had a flash lock built under its narrow pointed arches. The present bridge dates from 1825 although there was a construction over the river at this point for centuries. One report claims the first

Godstow: with the arrival of October visitors are less frequent, preferring their homes to the bleak river bank

was erected in 871 and there was certainly one in regular use in 1085.

Abingdon Bridge was built by the Fraternity of the Holy Cross in the fifteenth century to replace a popular ford which had been in use since 1416. It is in two sections, with an island in the centre. On the Berkshire side it is known as Abingdon Bridge; on the other as Burford Bridge. Abingdon Bridge was widened on the upstream side in 1828 with semi-circular arches, while Burford Bridge was altered and modified in 1927 when it was found to be partly unsound.

Chiswick: Late afternoon as a pale golden October sun strikes
the low water mark on the Upper Mall stretch of the river

It is known that there was a bridge at Shillingford in the fourteenth century, although the present triple-arched construction was built in 1827. This superseded a notoriously flimsy bridge, built of wood on stone piers and constructed in 1784 to replace a ferry. An earlier bridge was causing problems to users as far back as 1300. It was for many years also a popular fording place, as was Wallingford where the oldest part of the present bridge is thirteenth-century. It was repaired and widened after serious floods in the area in 1909.

Wallingford Bridge always had problems. Repairs were never adequate and there were many accidents. Numerous grants were made through the years to try to put things right and in 1530 five land arches were built. In 1646 four river arches were removed and replaced with a wooden drawbridge during the defence of the town; these were replaced with brick and stone arches in 1751. After flood damage the river arches were replaced by the three existing eliptical arches.

There has been a bridge at Streatley since the thirteenth century, at one time a chapel being included in the structure. The old bridge lasted until 1869 when it was taken down and a new crossing of wrought and cast iron with lattice-work girders opened. In 1926 this was replaced by the present concrete bridge.

There were originally timber bridges across the river at Reading, but the present structure, built in 1923, was at the time a tremendous engineering achievement, the great concrete arch spanning 180 ft. Sonning Bridge was also originally of timber. There has been a crossing here since at least Saxon times and the existing brick construction dates from 1604.

There are records of a bridge at Henley in 1230 and the present one was built with stone from Headington, near Oxford, in 1786, replacing one washed away by floods in 1774. It features sculptured heads of Father Thames and Isis on the keystones of the central arch, the work of the Hon. Mrs Damer, a relative of Horace Walpole. The five-arched bridge is often described as the 'noblest' on the Thames. Maidenhead had a timber bridge from the early seventeenth century but it was replaced by one designed in 1772 by Sir Robert Taylor. Oak from Windsor Forest was used to repair Windsor Bridge in the thirteenth century but there are records showing a permanent construction here since 1172, possibly to provide a Windsor–London link. The present cast-iron bridge, on a different site, dates from 1824. At one time tolls were imposed not only on traffic using the bridge but also on barges passing beneath it.

Nearby are the Victoria and Albert Bridges, opened in 1851 and replacing one at Datchet, where there was once a busy ferry. Bridges here have always suffered problems. In 1706 Queen Anne had one built; it was rebuilt in 1770 but in just over twenty years had collapsed. The ferry was brought back after this disaster until a new bridge was constructed in 1812. Again difficulties arose, with pieces frequently falling into the river. The trouble was that it had been built by separate authorities on opposite sides of the bank, with different materials and at different levels.

William IV and Queen Adelaide opened Staines Bridge in 1832, close to the site of previous bridges, including one dating from Roman times. There was an old timber bridge here until 1796, when a stone bridge was built alongside. However cracks were soon noticed in the arch and the timber construction came back into use until a replacement was built in 1807.

Another bridge with a history of continual problems was at Chertsey, where the existing bridge was built between 1780 and 1785, close to

On a November day a visitor views the river from this most famous vessel next to the nautical college

where there had been crossings since the early fourteenth century. It had to be partially rebuilt less than ten years after its opening. Designed by John Paine MP, it cost far more than originally anticipated mainly because neither end reached the banks!

One of the most unusual bridges along the Thames was built at Walton in 1750. It had an oriental appearance due to lattice timber work so arranged that damaged parts could be replaced at little cost. Its stone piers were later incorporated into a new design with four brick arches, but in

HAMPTON
A pale sun breaks through a November mist as the boats are made ready for the Winter in a riverside boatyard

All the year round the capital's waterway is alive. Here, on a November afternoon, boats are prepared for their trade

1859 the central arch collapsed and a new iron crossing was built five years later.

Beautiful Hampton once claimed to have one of the ugliest bridges on the river. Its first bridge, opened in 1753, was of timber but it did not last long and twenty-five years later it was replaced by an eleven-arched construction, also of wood. In 1866 an iron bridge was built but no one liked its appearance or the tolls imposed. These were lifted in 1876, but not until 1933, when the present lovely bridge, designed by Sir Edwin Lutyens, was opened by Edward, Prince of Wales, was the old eyesore removed.

Kingston Bridge is one of the most historically interesting sites along the Thames, as it was crossed by several Saxon kings. Built in the thirteenth century, it was until the eighteenth century the second Thames bridge from the sea. It was often in a poor condition and in 1377 Edward III gave authority for tolls to be levied on craft passing underneath. The design was later modified to receive drawbridges, but these severely weakened the structure and major improvements and repairs had to be carried out. The bridge was closed for a time after partly collapsing in 1814 but was rebuilt and opened by the Duchess of Clarence (later Queen Adelaide) in 1828. It had to be closed again early this century for widening.

Tower Bridge is London's best known bridge and one of its most famous landmarks. Its central span is formed by two drawbridges that are raised several times a day to allow ships to pass to and from the Pool of London. It is the farthest downstream of the Thames bridges and was opened in 1894. London Bridge, built just over fifty years earlier, was transferred, stone by stone, to become an unusual tourist attraction in the desert of Arizona, USA.

The River Thames has many fine bridges, but the masterpiece designed for Maidenhead by the engineer–inventor Isambard Kingdom Brunel as part of his plan for the Great Western Railway line from London to Bristol, must rate as one of the most impressive constructions spanning the water. Its brick arches are the widest and flattest in the world. Each span is 128 ft with a rise of only 24 ft. Brunel, son of Marc Isambard Brunel, a French-born inventor and engineer, was still a teenager when working with his father on the planning of a tunnel under the Thames from Wapping to Rotherhithe which was constructed between 1825 and 1843. When he was appointed engineer to the GWR he was still only twenty-seven, yet he convinced everyone he could produce the cheapest and best rail system. Before the work could get under way a Bill had to be passed by Parliament – the Great Western Railway Bill – in which it was proposed to start the line at both ends simultaneously between London and Reading and Bristol and Bath.

It was a gigantic undertaking, with an army of railway navvies living with their families in rough huts at the side of the track. It could also be dangerous, but Brunel said he was never prepared to send his men to work where he was not prepared to go himself and it is reported that on more than one occasion he used his athletic capabilities as a strong swimmer to rescue men trapped in flooded tunnels. The Paddington to Taplow section was opened in 1838 and the latter remained the western terminus for more than a year while the bridge was constructed at Maidenhead. Controversy surrounded the project, as the Thames authorities would not allow anything to obstruct the navigation channel of the river. Consequently Brunel was faced with designing a bridge with only one river support and a rise of only 24 ft was allowed for the highest points of its two arches. Many were convinced the bridge

A seasonal October day as a pale sun, still with some warmth, brings life to a sleepy boatyard

would fall down before it was completed as never before had anyone attempted to build such a shallow arch. But by October 1838 the construction work was over and the first engine to run over the bridge was Stevenson's 'North Star' which was taken on a barge to Maidenhead and unloaded 200 yd from the site chosen for Brunel's viaduct. Three lengths of track were placed on the road and moved one in front of the other. The engine was then moved to Taplow to await a trial run. Just over 8 miles of track were laid between Maidenhead and Twyford and traffic started to

MAIDENHEAD
Boatyards up and down the river pause during September, before the start of the Winter's maintenance work

GODSTOW
The lengthening shadows and the quality of light on an Autumn morning mark the approach of Winter on the upper Thames

roll in July 1839.

The two spans over the river are flanked on either side by four narrower arches and on one a commemorative plaque has been fitted to record the engineering feat. From Twyford the line was extended to Sonning where a cutting 2 miles long and 60 ft deep had been excavated. Brunel took over the work personally and with a workforce of 1,220 navvies and 196 horses overcame persistent flooding problems to see the first train go through to Reading in March 1840.

Brunel also planned the branch line from Windsor to Slough, at the request of Queen Victoria. Supporting the line either side of the Thames is a long, curving viaduct, which has 150 arches 10 ft high. These are joined by a suspension bridge to the arches on the Windsor bank which continue opposite the main gates of Windsor Castle. At Moulsford Brunel designed a bridge sweeping across the river at an angle, but with twisted arches to allow the piers to be set straight in the stream. His Thames bridges are the work of a genius; but it may have been all too much for him, for he died in 1859, only ten years after the death of his father.

T he River Thames is probably one of the world's great untapped treasure troves. How many secrets remain hidden in its muddy depths is unknown. Numerous discoveries of both major and minor importance have been made at regular intervals through the years, but there can be little doubt that these are

For centuries seafarers have set sail from this famous Greenwich riverside point. Now, on a November day, commuters travel on one of the many river buses

but a fraction of what could come to light. At one time Thames Conservancy offered a 10s reward to staff finding anything of antiquarian interest in or near the river, because it was realized that some items were being taken home as souvenirs and many ended up forgotten. What makes an ideal paperweight to one person provides a missing link in a chapter of history to another.

'Mudlarking', searching the river banks at low water, has been a popular pastime for Londoners for generations. Not a week passes without the

CHELSEA
Summer seems a long time ago on a cold November evening, but inside the houseboats it is warm and cosy

discovery of old Thames Conservancy licence plates, boat names, clay pipes, bottles. Some of the most collected items are pot lids which covered containers popular in Victorian times for holding pastes and cosmetics.

It is by dredging that several finds of importance have been found. Charles Roach Smith used to sit for hours and watch dredgers at work and then sift through the contents of the buckets. The British Museum has one of his prized discoveries. One day he noticed a bronze object in a bucket; he could not identify it, but kept it in his possession. Exactly a year later, at the same spot, he noticed another piece of bronze. It was identified as a Roman bronze peacock, minus its tail. The first piece he had found was the missing tail!

The valuable part that dredging can play was shown in 1955 when Thames Conservancy dredged an area at Staines close to where it is thought a Roman bridge crossed. The Romans called Staines '*Pontes*' ('bridges') and it was a great trading centre and important for transferring supplies destined for Silchester. The Romans built an inn and posting house close to the crossing and it was always thought a strong possibility that the river contained items of archaeological interest. Sure enough, the dredgers brought up various items of domesticity, especially Roman pottery.

The buckets also brought up bronze spear heads, Stone Age axe heads, Bronze Age utensils, centuries-old human bones, pewter tankards (which had presumably fallen overboard during regatta festivities) – and even a German machine gun. Many of the items are kept in the Thames Conservancy's collection at Reading Museum. Unfortunately, this collection has grown so large that it is impossible to put it on public display in its entirety. Important items found in the lower Thames invariably make their way to the British Museum and the Museum of London.

Much is still waiting to be discovered about primitive man who lived along the banks of the Thames 300,000 years ago. And how much evidence is waiting to come to the surface about the river's use as a commercial highway by the Romans, of the penetration by the Saxons, the activities of the Normans? Many items that have fallen into, or have been abandoned in, the river have perished, but it is certain that much has been preserved in the deep mud. Archaeologists anticipate that as development work progresses in the heart of London, much will come to light to give fresh evidence of the great industry which went on in the capital at the time of the Romans who built quays and warehouses to build up trade to the continent and to ship materials up and down the river. Although materials were shipped in a variety of craft it has always remained a disappointment that few of their remains have yet been found.

In 1962, however, an exciting discovery was made near Blackfriars – a sunken barge containing ragstone which originated from Kent. Its date can be accurately pin-pointed to the ninth century AD, because a coin of that date was found in the mast instep, a good luck ritual observed by boatbuilders.

Hand axes have been found in great number all

MILL END
The water which has come over the weir turns white with anger on a November day

A pale September sun plays on the front of the picturesque mill at Hambleden as Autumn takes over from Summer

along the river, including tools from the Palaeolithic period (300,000–8,000 BC) in gravel workings along north bank tributaries. A Bronze Age (1,800–550 BC) hunting spear head was found at Shifford and another at Surbiton; a sword of the same age came out of the river at Platt's Eyot, Hampton, and a flint axe from nearby Garrick's Ait; a New Stone Age flint sickle was found at Monkey Island, Bray, dating from 3,200 BC; and at nearby Bray Lock a Bronze Age spear head.

Stone and Bronze Age implements and pottery have been discovered at Streatley; Iron Age remains at Sunbury; Roman remains at Whitchurch. Thousands of coins have been found. Some of the stone axes have been made from stone foreign to the area, originating in Cornwall and the north of England. An axe head discovered at Bell Weir, near Runnymede, for example, was found to be made from stone identical to that observed at a New Stone Age camp in the Lake District.

Although all these finds are interesting, they are regarded by archaeologists as run-of-the-mill discoveries as far as the River Thames is concerned. At regular intervals an item of special interest causes excitement worldwide. Such an item was a 41 cm bust of Hadrian, the Spanish-born Roman emperor, dredged from the river near London bridge in 1834. Its original site is unknown, but it may have come from the London Forum which is believed to have been constructed around the period of Hadrian's reign from AD 117–138. The bust can be seen in the British Museum.

A bronze scabbard found at Fulham has decorated scrolls and a scene depicting the famous story of the wolf suckling Romulus, son of Mars and legendary founder and first king of Rome, and his twin brother Remus. The handle is missing, but the iron blade is contained within the scabbard. It is also in the British Museum, as is a bronze coolus helmet found in the river in London. It has the names of four owners on the neck guard and dates from around AD 43.

Another find in London were bronze forceps probably used during rites associated with Cybele,

TEDDINGTON

The river bank is home for large and small craft alike. With the arrival of September many will stay moored until next Summer

the Great Mother Goddess, and Attis, a Phrygian god, who castrated himself after being unfaithful. Another interesting find (Museum of London) is a Roman jug found at Southwark. It is inscribed *Londinii Ad Fanum Isidis* (At London at the Temple of Isis) and may have originated from a tavern in the first or second century AD. It is one of the earliest examples of an inscription using the Roman name for London.

There is a strong possibility that the river still holds a vast armoury – remnants of battles along the banks and other items thrown in the water on ceremonial occasions. Some swords and weapons discovered have been deliberately distorted by their owners before being discarded in this way. Weapons have been found which throw light on Saxon penetration along the river as far as Dorchester and of the discovery of the Thames by the Vikings who created havoc as they explored the route, looting monasteries of their treasure and killing vast numbers of the population.

There are many museums displaying items found in or close to the river. Some of the finest pieces can be seen at the British Museum in London; the London Museum in Kensington Palace; and Reading Museum. There are also museums of interest to those seeking further historical information about the River Thames. Of particular interest is the National Maritime Museum in Greenwich Park in south-east London. It illustrates and preserves the maritime history of Britain, covering the Royal Navy, merchant shipping, commercial fishing and pleasure sailing, with the use of models, pictures,

Staines: leaves turn golden, and a swan preens itself to make ready for the Winter

photographs, dioramas and life-sized displays of men at work, tools, ships' gear and relics and full-sized boats.

The London Underwater Museum is situated on the *MV Celtic Surveyor*, a 1930s P & O ferry berthed in West India Dock. Its displays include ancient and modern diving equipment, salvaged treasures and artifacts, among them items from the *Mary Rose*. Another floating museum is the *Cutty Sark*, the last of the China Tea Clippers, built in 1869, which attracts more than 400,000 visitors annually to its berth at King William

LONDON
Looking across to the Houses of Parliament from Lambeth Embankment as the November winds lay a carpet of leaves

Near to where once King John signed the Magna Carta at Runnymede, the mists of Autumn swirl on a grey day

Walk, Greenwich. Its permanent displays include the famous Long John Silver figurehead collection. Also at Greenwich is the Greenwich Borough Museum, with exhibitions of prehistory and history relating to the environment of the area.

Another floating attraction is HMS *Belfast* at Symons Wharf, off Tooley Street, London SE1. This 11,500 tonne cruiser is part of the Imperial War Museum. During World War Two it was one of the most powerful cruisers afloat and took part in the last battleship action in European waters.

And afloat in St Mary Overy Dock, Southwark, is *Kathleen May*, Britain's last remaining wooden three-masted topsail schooner, built in 1900. A coastal sailing trade exhibition is on board. Also of note are Blake's Lock Museum, Reading, which has displays of the history, industry and commercial life of the town and takes a look at the development of its waterways; and the Museum of English Rural Life, Reading, a national collection of material relating to the history of the countryside.

Autumn may see a sudden drop in the numbers enjoying the attractions of the River Thames, but the work of its watchdogs never ends. September 1989 represented a turning point in the history of environment protection in England and Wales, for on that day the National Rivers Authority started its duties. Overnight it became the strongest environmental protection agency in Europe, invested with extensive powers and responsibilities by Parliament.

The responsibilities of the NRA are far-reaching. Foremost is the control of pollution and improvement of the quality of Great Britain's river systems and coastal waters. This is to be achieved by raising environmental awareness within industry, commerce, farming and among the public, and by enforcing strict standards of environmental control. A balance must be struck between all the competing interests that use the rivers, while at the same time providing the

LONDON
The once busy power station at Battersea is still a landmark and is best seen from the river, as here on an October day

strongest possible protection for plant and animal life.

The Thames Region of the NRA is one of ten regional units and its aim is to safeguard the total river environment, not just the rivers, streams and lakes in the area, but also the quality and quantity of underground water. Regulating the rivers and groundwaters is only part of its work, however. It has the responsibility for the region's flood defence, for protecting and improving fish stocks, and for promoting water-based recreation. It has a vast area to cover. The Thames Region has a resident population of 11 million and covers 5,000 square miles, from Cirencester in the west to Dartford in the east and from Luton in the north to the Surrey Downs in the south. It includes 3,230 miles of rivers and 450 sites of special scientific interest and has to cope with 8,000 planning applications and development enquiries a year.

Three committees with membership drawn from local and national bodies, assist and provide direct channels of communication for interested parties: a Regional Flood Defence Committee, Regional Fisheries Advisory Committee and Regional Rivers Advisory Committee. Its activities are financed from a combination of local government precepts, direct charges and Government grant aid, and its policy is to recoup the maximum possible proportion of its costs directly from those who benefit. The Authority intends to invest more than £20 million on capital projects every year, with operating expenditure in the region of £35 million.

The sign of the floods of past years, on the lock-keeper's house at Henley

So what is happening in the Thames Region? Pollution control is seen as a vital part of the work. A sound knowledge of the chemical and biological processes is being built up, standards being drawn up for each stretch of river so that these can be taken into account when deciding whether to allow additional discharges. Teams of pollution control staff monitor major watercourses on a regular basis, water samples being regularly tested by laboratories. Their aim is to prevent pollution reaching the watercourses. If it does, immediate steps are taken to clear it as

LONDON
The tall buildings in the city rise into the chilly November air, leaving the cold river below

A bright November sun makes a pattern of shadows on Lambeth pier in the centre of the capital

proposed land developments and advize local authorities on any flood problems these may create. They carry out studies to discover the source of existing problems and to identify how best to cope with changing land use within each river catchment. When necessary engineers will design flood defence measures and oversee their construction.

From the region's flood control rooms a round-the-clock watch is kept on weather conditions and river levels. Staff interpret all information and give emergency services early warning of possible floods. Flood defence teams are based at site offices around the region to carry out regular river maintenance work. Activities range from dredging, weedcutting and removal of blockages to the maintenance and operation of the Thames Barrier and London's other tidal defences. These teams are mobilized during flood emergencies to keep rivers clear of obstructions so that flood waters can be conveyed away as quickly as possible.

A specialist staff encourages the development of a natural healthy river system, both above and below the water line, and provides expert advice to ensure the region's activities are carried out in an environmentally sensitive way. River maintenance is planned in detail and further advice is offered on when best to cut weeds, dredge river beds and trim banks and trees. At the same time, additional conservation measures embrace the planting of reed beds for wildlife habitats and ensuring any new structures such as bridges and weirs blend in with the local environment.

A thriving fish population is a sign of a healthy

quickly as possible and to issue warnings. Where appropriate, booms of absorbent material are placed in the water to trap floating pollutants, such as petrol and oils.

The prospect of flooding either from heavy rainfall or from abnormally high tides in the Thames Estuary is of prime concern. The Thames Barrier is discussed later, but reducing the risk of flooding on a day-to-day basis and planning major flood defence projects form a huge part of the region's work and involve more than half its manpower. Flood defence staff keep a check on

LONDON
The strong light of a November day warms and brings hidden colours to the stonework along the Albert Embankment

river, so fishery staff carry out surveys to determine the number and condition of fish, re-stock watercourses and monitor the health of fish moved by angling clubs. Often staff are called in to rescue fish in distress, either as a result of natural causes such as low oxygen levels in rivers during hot weather, or from pollution incidents, or to offer expert advice on a wide range of fishery management problems.

All this is the work of professionals. There are many others who take an active part in keeping an ever open eye on the Thames, among them the River Thames Society which has over two thousand members living all along the river who have formed their own branches. They take note of despoilation, not only on the water and along its banks but to adjacent buildings. Members see their most important task as providing an on-the-spot watch of all matters affecting the river. They keep an eye on planning applications ranging from helicopter pads, maintenance of stone stairs, housing projects and bridge work to commercial activity.

Proposed development of listed buildings is also carefully watched, together with the introduction of what are regarded as unsightly hotels and supermarkets. Members are particularly keen to ensure that footpaths and riverside walks are not engulfed by new development that threatens to restrict views of the river. A special tow-paths committee offers advice on the siting of riverside seats at locks and footbridges over the river. A close link has been established with the Port of London Authority in giving early warning of driftwood debris.

Boats are put away on an October day as the boys of Eton College turn to indoor sports

The question of pollution is an on-going problem for members and all branches keep constant watch for examples, whatever the source. One of the major pollution issues concerns the application by Thames Water for temporary relaxation of the consent relating to the discharges of sewage effluent.

Aware that keeping a boat on the river is a new experience for many, the River Thames Society regularly offers advice on what it describes as 'just good housekeeping' to those who lay up their boats in the Autumn or Winter and do not use

CAVERSHAM
The visitors are gone and soon the river will take on a Wintery aspect

London: sunset over the now quiet river of Autumn

them again until the Spring. This is the time of year when it is important to inspect the hull for damage or deterioration; to clean craft top to bottom; to ensure everything is watertight; to strip boats of all valuables; remove foodstuffs; check the engine; remove gas bottles; disconnect and drain the domestic water system and service the toilets; check fire extinguishers, and so on. Experienced boat-owners follow all these instructions, and carry out one hundred and one other tasks, automatically. But many others do not and as a result are plagued with problems once they take to the water again in the Spring. Another

problem facing some is the discovery that their craft have been broken into and vandalized. Society members operate a 'Winter-watch' scheme to try to prevent this happening.

The River Thames Society, which was formed in 1962, claims it is the only organization covering all interests from the source to the sea and has seven branches. Thames Head covers the stretch from source to Radcot; the others are Upper Thames (Radcot to Mapledurham); Middle Thames (Mapledurham to Windsor); Teddington to Old Windsor; Upper Tideway (Teddington to Putney Bridge); Central Tideway (Putney Bridge to Blackfriars Bridge); and Lower Tideway (Blackfriars Bridge to the Estuary).

A ripple of excitement mixed with surprise and a certain amount of disbelief was expressed in 1974, when for the first time for many years a salmon was recovered from the river-intake screens of West Thurrock Power Station. When records were checked it was discovered that such an occurrence had not taken place for 140 years. Up to this point biologists had already noticed a marked increase in the number of different fish species found in the estuary. There were only three in 1964 yet during a ten year period this figure had jumped to seventy-five. This proved conclusively that the estuary was recovering from its previously polluted state.

Since that time work has been undertaken to test the feasibility of salmon returning to the

LONDON
It may not be a leafy towpath, but these two anglers still enjoy an afternoon's fishing in November

Thames. A pilot study was initiated in 1979, the first phase running for seven years and involving the recruitment of two salmon fishery experts. Initially they identified sites in the tributaries where juvenile salmon could thrive. Various parameters were examined, including water quality, depth, flow, flood sources, predation and angling pressure. After selecting the sites the scheme was explained to landowners to ensure their full co-operation before stocking with salmon parr (young salmon) purchased from commercial fish farms. This stocking continues, but is now carried out with fish provided very largely as gifts from the salmon farming industry.

To help identify these young 'Thames' salmon a small vestigial fin, the adipose, was removed and in additional tests some of the parr were tagged by implanting a minute piece of binary coded wire into the snout of the fish. The microtags can be detected electronically with special equipment and contribute to international efforts to identify the origins of salmon caught in the high seas fisheries as well as building up information on the Thames itself.

When they are ready to migrate the parr undergo changes to prepare them for life at sea. They become silvery and are known as smolt. In parallel with parr stocking, smolts are stocked at sites further downstream. The smolt stage is very important because this is the time at which the young salmon fix the 'scent' of their home river in their memory.

Since 1979 the number of parr and smolts released annually has averaged 61,000 and 14,000 respectively. The survival of the stocked parr is calculated to be about 9 per cent in the seven best nursery streams. The total migration from stocked parr is therefore between 3,000–5,000 a year. This increases the total annual downstream run of smolts to around 16,000.

The next stage of the project was to monitor the number of adults returning after their time at sea, a period which can vary between one and three years. The run of the returning fish probably starts as early as April or May, but the first salmon are not generally seen until June or July. The main means of monitoring the returning salmon is the salmon 'trap' at Molesey Weir, which works on the principle of attracting the salmon to a fast flow of water whereupon they swim into a holding pool for later tagging, examination and release above the weir.

Electro-fishing, a harmless process in which the fish are stunned, counted and once recovered returned to the river, is carried out in shallow water. Information supplied by anglers and members of the public is also noted. All of these methods have their limitations in accuracy, but the best estimates of the number of fish returning showed that an average of 100 fish per annum returned between 1982 and 1985. In 1986 this had increased to 175.

The last stage of the work undertaken during this feasibility study was experimentation with artificial propagation from salmon that had been successfully grown in, and returned to, the Thames. The reasoning behind this was that by using a returning fish, genetic selection would

LONDON
Futuristic buildings rise where once the traditional docks thrived and bustled

produce offspring more adept at withstanding the unique conditions in the river.

To undertake this work fish captured in the late Autumn were retained in tanks. In November these fish were artificially spawned or stripped. Approximately 1,200 eggs per kilogram of female body weight were obtained and these were immediately mixed with the milt of two males to ensure maximum fertilization. The eggs were then incubated and the fry raised by two outside organizations as the authority does not have the facilities to do this itself.

Since 1982 an average of 49,000 ova have been obtained and about 4,000 smolts and parr restocked each year. This rate of production is insufficient to support even the restocking programme of the first seven years. Work on artificial propagation is continuing and will do so until the salmon can return all the way up river to the nursery streams and spawn naturally.

Having proved that salmon could return to the Thames in reasonable numbers, the greatest remaining obstacle to success is the existence of the many weirs in the main river and tributaries. These make upstream migration either difficult or in many cases impossible. In 1986 a charity, the Thames Salmon Trust, was launched to encourage commercial sponsorship of a scheme to build salmon 'ladders' at the major weirs. The National Rivers Authority, Thames Region, is supporting the Trust's activities with financial contributions and by incorporating salmon 'ladders' in the design of new replacement weirs such as that completed at Goring. Eight of these ladders have so far been built, the most recent being at Sunbury.

KEMPSFORD
Early Winter in a quiet backwater, high on the upper river in the light of a December day

WINTER

Winter is icummen in,
Lhude sing Goddamm,
Raineth drop and staineth slop,
And how the wind doth ramm!

Ezra Pound

The boat hire companies have put up their shutters. The grass has stopped growing. The trees are bare. River mists affect birds hunting for prey. Some optimistic animals still forage for food. A bareness has come to the river. Seeds drift in the winds and float on top of the water. Fields become empty as cattle are tucked away for the Winter. Brown rats vacate their riverside haunts and head for the warmth of farm buildings.

December brings the shortest day and the sun has disappeared. Snow covers feeding grounds for wildlife, but for many it is not a worry as they have already retreated to their Winter quarters after a final addition to the insulation. Birds perch together for warmth, sitting puffed up side by side in a closeness which would have caused a fight in warmer weather. It is time to contemplate the threat of floods.

Farmers carry out work they did not have time for in the Summer, hedging and ditching, while re-sown fields begin to show life. Fine days are the time for boat maintenance, wet days to stand in a pub and recall your year on the river. It is the time for the mistletoe and for robins to sing out an announcement that they have found their Winter territory, and when wild mink become more active as they raid water birds and fish.

A very cold January morning as the early light comes up over the river bank on the border of Oxfordshire and Berkshire

LALEHAM
A February morning as the sun comes out between the showers, to light the river bank flooded by days of rain

Threats of serious flooding have rippled along the River Thames for thousands of years, although the earliest record of a major disaster is AD 9. Some forty years later thousands of acres were under water and deaths through drowning were estimated at 10,000. Ever since then floods have taken place with varying degrees of severity during the winter months, usually in November. Thirty were recorded before the Great Flood of 1894. It is no coincidence that many towns and villages are set away from the river.

An unexpected downpour, prolonged wet weather, rapid thaw, spring tides – all can change the river's pattern in a matter of hours. When many more people than today relied on the Thames for their livelihood, there was widespread hardship. They were not only put out of work but disastrous problems were encountered getting supplies from one point to another. Farmers and industrialists were hit hard.

Severe flooding was recorded along the river's banks in Oxfordshire in 1680, and the eighteenth century was also badly affected by floods. Flood water reached a depth of 7 ft 7 in at Long Wittenham in 1768. Six years later it was worse and Henley Bridge was carried away. In 1783 floods were reported again along the river's entire length and the following year there were similar problems when bargemen were prevented from working for two months.

In 1809 King George III was stranded at Windsor when Eton Bridge was washed away and several fords completely disappeared. In 1852 there was chaos at the Duke of Wellington's

The Winter sun warms willow trees next to the flooded Thames, as the river crosses from Gloucestershire to Wiltshire at Cricklade

funeral at Maidenhead, when the hearse and horses were swept over by flood water. Worse was to come in the nineteenth century, however. The Great Flood of 1894 struck in November, preceded by exceptional rainfall. The amount of rain falling during the twenty-six days prior to 17 November was almost a third of the total annual rainfall for the area – 8 in. Molesey was 8 ft 6 in above its normal Summer level; Bray was 8 ft 3 in higher; Romney 7 ft 8 in; Boveney 6 ft 2 in; Cookham 5 ft 10 in; Marlow 5 ft 9 in.

CASTLE EATON
December time, with the upper river high in flood over the banks across the fields near to St Mary's church

The fields under flood water, as the infant river runs between Cricklade and Lechlade after days of rain during December

Boatyards were flooded by an average of 4 ft of water, banks were washed away, cattle drowned, homes evacuated, roads cut off.

The famous playing fields of Eton disappeared from sight and the college was closed and its food store handed over to those in need. Traders attempted to deliver goods in small craft. Trains were suspended between Staines and Windsor. Queen Victoria was so concerned about the situation that she personally headed an appeal fund to help those affected, visited some of the hardest hit areas, and ordered that all transport be made available for relief work.

Thames Conservancy, which had expressed mounting concern about the threat from flooding in 1777, determined that such a disaster must not bring the Thames valley to a standstill again. Engineers worked out detailed schemes to construct new channels. But the threat was always there. Fourteen people died when central London was flooded in 1928 and disastrous floods in 1953 along the east coast and the Thames estuary cost three hundred lives. It was felt that had the floods reached the centre of the capital, with its highly populated low lying areas, the result could have proved a national catastrophe. It would not only have caused great loss of life but totally paralyzed the underground; knocked out fresh water and sewer systems together with gas, power and vital telephone and data systems; affected thousands of homes, shops, factories and business premises. It would have taken London several months to get back to normal and conservative estimates as to the amount of probable damage gave a figure of £3,500 million. What could be done?

A traditional solution to overcome flooding is to raise and strengthen river walls and embankments. Following the Thames Flood Act of 1879 stretches of the bank were dealt with in this way and again between 1930 and 1935. But the problem was increasing. It was possible to redevelop all riverside sites to incorporate high defences, but this would mar the beauty of London's riverline for the 27 million tourists who use the Thames to explore London each year, and it would take a long time.

THAMES BARRIER
Sunset over the Thames Barrier on a Winter's afternoon

What was causing great concern was the realization of a steady increase in tide levels caused by a combination of factors, including a tilting of the British Isles, with the south-eastern corner tipping downwards; settlement of London on its bed of clay; increasing mean sea levels and increasing tidal amplitude. It was found that high tide levels were rising in central London at the rate of 75 cm per century.

It was known that a particular threat was from the surge tides which take place when a trough of low pressure moves eastwards across the Atlantic towards Britain and the sea beneath rises above normal level, creating a 'hump' which moves eastwards with the depression. If the depression passes the north of Scotland and veers southwards extremely dangerous conditions may be created, and a surge takes place when the mass of water coming from the deep ocean reaches the shallow southern part of the North Sea. The height of such a surge may be further increased by strong northerly winds. These fears resulted in the construction of the Thames Barrier.

While appreciating that building what would be the world's largest movable flood barrier would not only be costly (£535 million, plus £3.3 million annually to cover operational and maintenance requirements) but also an engineering challenge of immense proportions, it was considered that this was the best possible solution. Sited across the river at Woolwich Reach, it could be built without too much delay and cause relatively little interference with river traffic. Royal Assent to the Thames Barrier and Flood Prevention Act was given in 1972, and construction started late in 1974. It became operable in October 1982, was first used in 1983, and was officially opened by the Queen the following year.

To improve London's defences against flooding while the main defences were under construction interim bank raising was started in 1971. Some 32 km of flood defences were built downstream of the barrier, with bank levels 2 m higher than before. Between 1971 and 1972 102 km of interim bank raising was carried out from Putney to Purfleet, including the 60 m high Barking Barrier which has a drop gate held out of the water when not in use to allow uninterrupted passage by commercial shipping using Barking Creek. Defences upstream of Putney on the south bank, and Hammersmith on the north, were also raised to give the same degree of protection as in central London and to reduce the risk of flooding when high upland flows coincide with high tides which are not sufficiently large to warrant a barrier closure.

As the work was carried out, the building of attractive river walks and other riverside improvements were put into action as part of the permanent bank reconstruction. Particular attention was also given to ensuring the continued potential of existing riverside commerce and industry.

How does the barrier work? Basically, the rising sector gate barrier is a series of separate movable gates positioned end to end across the river, each pivoted and supported between concrete piers which house the operating machinery and control equipment. Closing the barrier seals

Even on a cold January afternoon the Thames Barrier, built
to stop flooding, is one of London's major show pieces

each having a clear span of 61 m. The four main massive gates are each designed as a hollow steel plated structure over 20 m high and weighing, with counterweights, about 3,700 tonnes. Each gate is capable of withstanding an overall load of more than 9,000 tonnes.

The barrier is operated by a staff of just over sixty, and decisions to close the barrier are taken by the controller. Dangerous conditions can be forecast about twelve hours in advance from the predicted height of the incoming tide estimated by the East Coast Storm Tide Warning Service based at Bracknell, together with information from the barrier's own sophisticated computer analysis of the situation. Closure normally takes place about one hour after low water or about four hours before the peak of the incoming surge tide reaches the site. Before closing the barrier, staff inform the Port of London Authority, which then notifies shipping by radio. Illuminated notice boards are brought into action both upstream and downstream. The gates, controlled and powered from the southern shore, take just thirty minutes to close.

The complexities of the Thames Barrier have caught the imagination of people worldwide and today a visitors' centre is one of London's big attractions. It operates from the south bank and includes an informative exhibition and audio visual show explaining the history, construction and operation of the capital's tidal flood defences.

The Winter of 1989–90 gave clear evidence that flood dangers do not only approach from one direction, as water poured into the Thames from

off part of the upper Thames from the sea. When not in use the gates rest out of sight in curved recesses in concrete sills in the riverbed, allowing free passage of river traffic through the openings between the piers. If a dangerously high tidal surge threatens, the gates swing up through 90 degrees from the riverbed position, forming a continuous steel wall facing downriver ready to stem the tide. Further rotation of the gates to the maintenance position renders every part accessible. The width of the barrier from bank to bank is about 520 m with four main openings,

its tributaries following heavy rain over a prolonged period. Damage running into millions of pounds was caused to riverside properties from Oxford to Maidenhead.

Flooding has not been the only weather hazard along the river, of course. Droughts have created problems through the years and levels reached an all-time low in 1921. In the eighteenth century the water level was so low that many craft became stranded on shallows, and a century later another drought seriously affected barge work.

It has also been known for almost the entire river to be frozen over. The earliest record of such an occurrence appears to be AD 220 when such conditions persisted over a period of several months, and in AD 923 the river was frozen for thirteen weeks. In 1410 there was ice on the river for an even longer period.

Watermen and bargemen finding themselves temporarily out of work during such conditions in more recent years found it profitable to organize 'frost fayres' on the ice, when oxen were roasted and a variety of games played. At times the ice was so thick that it could bear the weight of large skating parties and light vehicles.

The Romans were the first to realize what a perfect highway the Thames was for trade. They built vast wharves on both banks, and shipped out corn, cattle, gold, silver, iron, hides, slaves and even hunting dogs. The Saxons were also quick to appreciate its value as a commercial route.

The river may be in flood, but on a February morning it is time to be on the bank fishing, despite the cold

Due to the deplorable condition of the roads, the river gradually developed into one of the principal transport routes in southern England, with an ever increasing variety of goods shipped from sites all along the river, from Lechlade to London. Shipbuilders built stronger and larger craft to meet an increasing demand as supplies were stock-piled during the Summer months to await the fast moving waters of the Winter. Given favourable conditions a large barge could travel 35 miles a day downstream, while those travelling upstream took longer, and their progress was

LONDON
The pale sun on a January afternoon looking from Waterloo Bridge to the city

The river bus moves away from the Festival Pier late on a
January afternoon as the day comes to its end

public wharf, while others were set up by local
businessmen.

The highest point upstream to witness hectic
trade was Cricklade, the only Wiltshire town on
the Thames, its name deriving from *Criccagelad*,
'Place of wharves or creeks where the river can be
crossed'. But Lechlade, a few miles downstream,
was a hive of commercial activity for centuries.

Lechlade takes its name from the River Leach
and from 'lade', meaning to load, to take on a
load. Wharves were built in ever increasing
number as packhorses and carts from many areas
made their way to the river. Trade in this small
town, already strong, received a considerable
boost in 1789 with the opening of the Thames and
Severn Canal. Convoys of packhorses made their
way along 'salt ways' with vast quantities of salt
from Droitwich. Local Gloucestershire cheese was
also in demand and Cotswold stone taken from
quarries near Burford was shipped to Oxford and
London. Some was used for rebuilding St Paul's
Cathedral.

Other trading centres of importance sprang up
along the Thames at Oxford, Wallingford, Reading, Henley, Hedsor, Maidenhead, Windsor,
Staines, Hampton and Kingston. Much of the
river traffic concentrated on the shipment of grain
from the many watermills. Other mills produced
animal feedstuffs, clay pipes, cloth, timber or
were involved in smelting and forging. Today
there is just one working example of a Thames
watermill, the fifteenth-century building at
Mapledurham which is back in operation after
costly restoration. Milling had been introduced

often assisted by armies of men and horses who
were hired to help with towing.

Barges carried grain from the Thames Valley;
cheese from Gloucestershire; Cotswold building
stone from West Oxfordshire; fruit from Wor-
cestershire; coal from Staffordshire and the Forest
of Dean; salt from Cheshire; wool from the Cots-
wolds; flour from scores of mills scattered along
the river; plus cement, newsprint and timber.
Trade continued to increase to such an extent that
almost every town and village established its own

OXFORDSHIRE
The flowers and visitors of Summer have gone. It is a cold day near Oxford as the river starts to snake across the flat farm land

along the Thames by the Romans and Saxons and had become a huge financial success, the early timber structures gradually being replaced by more permanent buildings as trade prospered. At the time of the Domesday survey there were almost 6,000 watermills in England, the biggest percentage being along the Thames.

Although the introduction of canals in the eighteenth century did much to increase Thames-based trading, commercially the river began to deteriorate a century later as roads improved and the railways penetrated the Thames Valley. Craft used exclusively for trading became idle and eventually began to disappear altogether from the non-tidal Thames. Yet today the river is the heart of a vast commercial empire, goods being sent around the world. The Port of Tilbury, exactly half-way between London and the estuary, is regarded as the best located port in Great Britain, possibly in Europe. Yet shortly after it opened in 1886 it was something of a financial disaster and its future was uncertain.

The Port of Tilbury's cargo handling activity is now divided into three operational divisions: containers, conventional and bulk grain. Engineering and dry dock facilities are also offered. Restructuring of the port following the abolition of the Dock Labour Scheme is seen to have created new opportunities both for management and customers and substantial new investment in plant and facilities has been carried out. Both in-dock and riverside berths are provided. The Bulk Grain Terminal, the Northfleet Hope Container Terminal and the London International Cruise Terminal

On a February afternoon Spring is not long away and it is time to look around, for soon the visitors will be back

are situated here. Berths in the enclosed docks are served by a lock measuring just over 304 m in length and have a constant minimum water depth of 11 m.

The container division has its own rail container terminal, with a daily service to all major industrial centres in Britain. Fully computerized – as are all the other departments at the port – it deals with exports and imports, the entire operation being carried out within a high security customs fence patrolled by the port's own police force.

Tilbury is also one of Great Britain's leading

Waiting for the ferry on the old pier at Tilbury on a dull
December day; once ships travelled the world from here

specialities, such as Far Eastern hardwoods.

The terminal handles timber and sheet materials as well as pulp, paper and newsprint. Specialist equipment handles the wide range of materials which are shipped as far afield as the Americas, Russia, Australasia and the Far East.

A recent £1.5 million expansion scheme at Peninsula Docks was carried out for bulk metals handling, offering shippers the fastest loading capacity in Europe. Other bulk operations with high performance equipment include cement, featuring one of the first floating facilities of its kind in Europe, with bulk delivery to road vehicles and a bagging and palleting facility.

More than one hundred passenger ships a year call at Tilbury's International London Cruise Terminal, the only one on the river which has its own Customs and Immigration facilities.

The purpose-built grain terminal is the largest in the UK, with the ability to handle import and export vessels. It has seen a rapid growth through the years because of Tilbury's location in relation to European and world markets and its proximity to East Anglia, the country's primary grain producing area. It has a 275 m jetty; 100,000 tonnes storage capacity; and is capable of handling cargoes of up to 65,000 tonnes discharging and 50,000 tonnes loading. Discharging is carried out via marine elevator towers, each of which is capable of dealing with 1,000 tonnes an hour. Grain is transferred to an adjacent silo on an enclosed high speed conveyor.

There is an inner jetty handling vessels of up to 137 m and up to 10,000 tonnes, offering a loading

conventional cargo ports. It offers a range of specialist facilities: forest products, general cargo, bulk metal, bulk cement, roll-on/roll-off and an international passenger terminal. The specialist berths dedicated to forest products constitute the largest purpose-built terminal in the country and account for almost 10 per cent of the total UK trade, annual throughput exceeding 1.5 million tonnes. Flexible facilities mean that Tilbury is able to accommodate the wide range of vessels involved in the forest products trade and can offer dedicated facilities for large users of particular

COALHOUSE
Looking out over the marshes, which have changed little for many centuries

TEMPLE
On a January day, the new footbridge and riverside path are quiet; in a few months time the visitors will be back

rate of 2,000 tonnes an hour. A separate coaster jetty is dedicated to vessels of up to 90 m, capable of an annual throughput of more than 2 million tonnes.

The Romans displayed a natural brilliance in boatbuilding and constructed craft of varying sizes for use on the Thames. They even built their own machinery to provide wharves, their ingenious inventions including pile drivers and drop hammers. The tradition started by them has been maintained through the centuries, and craft made along the Thames have been exported around the world. At one time there was probably not a navigational river in the British Isles which did not have a traditional Thames-built boat, or one designed along its banks.

The oldest known Thames craft is the Peter-boat, named after the patron saint of fishermen, which was used extensively for net fishing and was double ended and fitted with a wet wall. Larger versions had a spritsail and foresail. During the seventeenth and eighteenth centuries, however, the most popular craft on the Thames was the wherry, the forerunner of today's sleek pleasure boats. It was the first passenger-carrying boat on the Thames, despite its clumsiness. Built in clinker construction – timbers overlapped and were 'clinked' with copper nails and washers to hold them together – the wherry was pointed to both bow and stern. They were usually just under 30 ft long, with a beam of less than 6 ft, and could accommodate a maximum of eight passengers, plus luggage.

Looking over the north shore to Gravesend, as the pale January light picks out the southern shore and the river spreads out at low tide

Waterman were in charge of wherries, armed with sculls for short ferrying trips When longer journeys were planned it was customary for two watermen to share the workload, and even to extend the crew to three, one with sculls and two with oars. It is likely that ferry services were operated by wherries because they were reasonably reliable. Owning such a craft was a guarantee of regular employment as there was always something or someone waiting to be transported, since they were not only ideal for

Soon the river will awaken from the Winter; at the end
of February the sun warms this boatyard at Datchet

In 1555 the Watermen's Company was formed, and at the same time an apprenticeship scheme was introduced. Initially this ran for twelve months but it was extended to cover a seven year period. Anyone working a wherry on his own who had not served his full apprenticeship faced a £10 fine. Later the wherry operators were joined by the Lightermen's Company, the amalgamation resulting in the Company of Watermen and Lightermen of the River Thames and granted its own coat of arms by Elizabeth I.

The men took immense pride in their wherries and used them not only for work but for relaxation and sport, holding their own regattas. Official recognition of the part these boats played in the life of the Thames came in 1845 at Henley Regatta when a special race was held offering a model silver wherry as the prize. Five years later the prize became silver gilt cups and eventually the race was classified as the Silver Goblets, a name which is retained to this day.

Watermen also used punts for short commercial trips, fitting them with rowlocks and propelling them with a pair of sculls. Anglers also took a liking to punts and installed a wet wall running from side to side, and side gratings to allow water to flow through. Usually the craft were made with soft bottoms of pine to allow easy and cheap replacement when damaged in the shallows.

With the increasing popularity of punts, and their growing use as leisure craft, mainly because they were a cheap form of river transport, designs were modified, becoming lighter and more streamlined. Thames boatbuilders, always quick

moving items from one side of the river to the other, but also for carrying out assignments upstream and downstream and as supply carriers for houseboats.

Operating wherries was regarded as something of an honour by the watermen and they became the first public servants to wear a form of uniform, an instantly recognizable outfit consisting of pleated coat, knee breeches with hose and a cap with a stiff peak. Each waterman displayed an identification badge on his clothing, showing the name of his employer and licence number.

SONNING EYE
A cold wind blows across an old gravel pit next to the river at Sonning Eye, near Reading; soon February will make way for Spring

LONDON
On a December night the cold water reflects the light from Westminster Bridge and the Houses of Parliament

to react to the public's changing demands, began to make better punts, using mahogany, installing cushions and back rests for comfort, and adding decorative paint work and even carvings. To cope with the inclement weather, canvas hoods were introduced. The leisurely pace of river traffic was rapidly disappearing, however, and in spite of extra modifications designed to keep passengers dry as cruiser traffic increased the popularity of the punt gradually receded.

As more and more people looked on the river as somewhere to spend a holiday it became apparent that a large number were not content just to sit on the banks or walk along the tow-paths but wanted to get afloat. Early in the nineteenth century other types of craft began to appear in great numbers. The wherry was replaced by a gig, shorter but wider than the punt, then came the skiff, the popularity of which has hardly faltered although many today are made from glass-reinforced-plastic.

The dinghy became popular; shorter but wider than either gig or skiff, it was found to be easy to handle in all conditions. But they too began to disappear and few have been built on classic lines for well over half a century. Other craft in use included the shallop, which could be used by four oarsmen, sculling boats and several types of canoe.

The first steam-powered craft to become available for hire was the *Richmond* in 1814, named in honour of its home base. The popularity of these craft increased at such a rate that towards the end of the century Charles Dickens observed that

The toll bridge at Swinford, built in 1777, is one of two over the river which still make a charge

owners of such craft drove at an excessive speed, with utter disregard to other river users. In short, he said, 'they are an unmitigated nuisance'.

The Electric Power Storage Company of Millwall owned the first electric launch. Somewhat appropriately it was named *Electricity*. Larger passenger craft followed from a number of yards and some made their way to overseas waterways. In 1888 a Thames-built electric passenger boat was used to travel up and down the Danube during the Viennese Exhibition. Even electric canoes became a familiar sight.

Early in December, at the start of the Winter, the sun lights the reeds on the river bank at Frogmill

About this time petrol-driven craft were also becoming common on the Thames and by the turn of the century petrol/paraffin engines were developing and motor boats were gaining attention. The boatbuilders of the Thames continued to show their skill and ingenuity and the results of their experiments were snapped up as among the finest to be found anywhere in the country. With the outbreak of World War One these builders turned their hands to fast launches for the Royal Navy and for a time Thornycroft's Hampton yard proudly displayed a motor boat bearing the insig-

nia of the Victoria Cross. The Coastal Forces boat had achieved fame by sinking the cruiser *Oleg* in 1918 in the Baltic, an action which had resulted in its commander receiving the award. Thornycroft's, later to become Vospers, produced well over a hundred of these boats for the Navy. Its yards were again active in World War Two, specializing in speedy torpedo and gun boats.

Then, of course, there is the good old Thames tug. The first steam tug to appear on the Thames was the *Lady Dundas* in 1832, built on the River Tyne. In later years, however, others were constructed along the Thames, particularly those fitted with diesel engines. Most popular crafts today are modern motor boats with glass-reinforced-plastic hulls and luxury cabins that would grace many apartments.

Many have been saddened to see the disappearance of some of the older boats of the Thames, and in 1980 a group of enthusiasts formed the Thames Traditional Boat Society to restore old boats, including skiffs, dinghies, punts and canoes and to keep them in regular use. The Thames Vintage Boat Club's 160 members own mostly Edwardian powered craft, and its members spend their Winters doing their own restoration work. Interest in steam-powered craft is fostered through the Steamboat Association of Great Britain.

The quiet of Winter provides a perfect time to explore the majestic – and in some cases historic – buildings to be found within easy

OXFORD
A pale Winter's day as the river runs through the city; in the months to come the punts will be back

reach of the river Thames.

London itself has a wealth of triumphs in stone, but there are many outstanding properties by the side of the river as it penetrates the counties westwards. Several deserve greater recognition. But whereas in the capital one can be overwhelmed by architectural splendour every few yards in certain areas, out in the shires are treasures so tucked away that they are frequently completely overlooked.

Within twenty miles of the source stands Buscot Park, an eighteenth-century mansion run by the National Trust, with an internationally acclaimed collection of paintings and furniture. Its park and water garden stands amid an area of farmland and woods running down to the Thames and it is a comparatively undiscovered gem. It has a most extraordinary history, being the scene of advanced pioneering farming methods in the nineteenth century. Bricks made here were shipped down river from a specially-built wharf and close to Buscot Lock was a distillery which produced beetroot brandy that was even exported to France! The Adam-style house, which is open to the public, has lakes and gardens laid out by Harold Peto.

Nearby is Kelmscott Manor, regrettably all too infrequently available for public viewing. It was here that William Morris lived for many years and when he died in 1896 he was buried in the local churchyard. Morris, writer, craftsman, artist and socialist visionary, did much of his work in this Tudor manor situated on the upper Thames floodplain and here there is a museum devoted to his work.

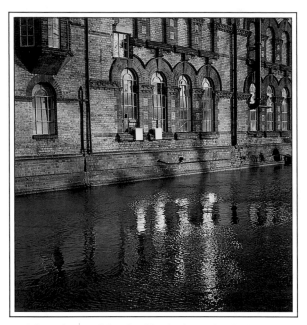

A December sun lights the side of a factory beside the river at Oxford

Oxfordshire has much to offer. At Henley is the sixteenth-century Grey's Court (National Trust) with its medieval ruins, beautiful gardens and Tudor donkey wheel for running water; near at hand is Fawley Court, designed and built by Wren in 1684 and decorated by Grinling Gibbons and James Wyatt, with its gardens the work of Capability Brown. Close to the town's bridge is Chantry House, dating from the fourteenth century and the oldest building in the town.

Further downstream towards Reading is Maple-

THE POOL OF LONDON
Old warehouses on the river front on a December morning, now homes for city workers

MEDMENHAM
The sun on a February day lights the stone of the fine old Abbey, where the Hellfire Club met in the 1700s

Late on a January afternoon the light goes down on the mill at Mapledurham, one of the oldest surviving Thames corn mills

durham, which has been in the same family since it was built in the sixteenth century, and which boasts its original moulded ceilings, great oak staircase, paintings, private chapel built under special licence, and restored fifteenth-century water mill. Alexander Pope was a frequent visitor here and enjoyed nothing more than walking through the grounds sweeping down to the river.

Clearly seen from the river is Medmenham Abbey between Henley and Marlow. This old Cistercian monastery was the meeting place of the infamous Hell Fire Club founded by Sir Francis Dashwood of West Wycombe in 1745 and the scene of black magic and orgies.

Nearer Marlow is the imposing Bisham Abbey, now a Sports Council centre, which was built on the site of an Augustinian Monastery and has links with the Knights Templars. Queen Elizabeth I stayed here, but it also lays claim to one of the best recorded ghost stories of the Thames. The spirit in question is said to be that of the wife of Sir Edward Hoby, who murdered her small son in a burst of temper when she was dismayed at his educational abilities. Years after these ghostly tales began to circulate, school books written in a childish hand and badly blotted were discovered on the premises.

Another jewel to glitter close to the Thames is Eton College, its chapel, dining hall, and the east and west sides of the cloisters remaining from the original building constructed during the reign of Henry VI. Not far away is Cliveden, now a luxury hotel, whose sale by the Duke of Westminster in 1883 to an American millionaire, William Astor, so grieved Queen Victoria.

It is the riverside properties in and around London, however, which are the most visited in the country: the Tower of London, built as a fortress in the reigns of William I and William II to control London; the Greenwich Museum complex, the finest architectural group in the capital; the Palace of Westminster, where the Houses of Parliament have met for centuries; the part twelfth-century residence of the Archbishop of Canterbury beside Lambeth Bridge; Hampton Court, where Cardinal Wolsey founded his enormous palace in

WAPPING BASIN
A January morning; just one of the many old buildings which line the area of the old docks

Wapping: down to the river in the old docks

On a day in January, not many visitors pass the sign to the lock and river bank at Hurley

the early sixteenth century. Then there is Windsor, the largest inhabited castle in the world.

Lesser-known properties on London's riverside include great Queen Anne and Georgian houses in Chelsea, once a pleasant Tudor village. Scottish author Thomas Carlyle lived in Cheyne Row for forty-seven years and entertained some of the leading Victorian authors, among them Dickens, Thackeray, Browning and Tennyson.

Rosetti, painter and poet, lived in nearby Tudor House, where Swinburne also stayed for a time; George Eliot lived in the same area; Sir Thomas

More was an earlier resident. Charles II built a house here, now home to the Chelsea Pensioners. Whistler lived in Cheyne Walk for more than ten years, frequently painting local scenes. Take a close look at Crosby Hall in Cheyne Walk – it was once in Bishopsgate. It formed part of a much larger building constructed in 1466 but was severely damaged by fire in the seventeenth century. The remaining structure was transferred to Chelsea and rebuilt on the site of Sir Thomas More's garden. It was a building that obviously caught the attention of Shakespeare, being mentioned in his *Richard III*.

Along the Thames in London you will also find the Blewcoat School at Westminster (National Trust), built in 1709 at the expense of a local brewer for the private education of poor children and continuing as an educational establishment until 1926. Hogarth House, Chiswick, was home to the artist for fifteen years; and Kensington Palace, built by William II in 1689, was altered and added to by Sir Christopher Wren. All along the Thames are buildings to stir the imagination: Thackeray went to school at Walpole House, which many believe to have provided the original for Miss Pinkerton's establishment for young ladies in *Vanity Fair*; Ham House, Richmond (National Trust), built about 1610, is one of the best examples of Stuart monastic architecture. There is much more to the Thames than liquid history.

The fishermen fill the river banks during the cold days of Winter, like this one in February at Medmenham

The Thames Path, the first part of which opens this year, will run from Ewen to the Thames Barrier, and can be enjoyed at all seasons. It is the fourteenth official long distance route in England and Wales – and the first to cover the course of a river.

A year after the idea was announced in 1984 a Thames Path Project Officer began the mammoth task of consulting with local authorities, land-owners and other interested parties on the full implications of a path covering 290 km (180 miles). The planned opening date is to be late 1994 or early 1995, but with access problems to be sorted out in London, the path is unlikely to be fully operational before 2010.

Such a path will not only provide an attractive visual amenity and leisure route for an ever increasing army of walkers but will also attract cyclists and horseriders. Three lengths have so far been proposed for cycleway status: Runnymede to Eton Bridge; Sonning Bridge to Caversham Bridge, Reading; and Donnington Bridge to God-stow Bridge, Oxford. The needs of the disabled are also being taken into consideration when working out access points. To ensure maximum

FROGMILL
A fine old boat on the river bank between Henley and Marlow on a December day

HENLEY
A late February afternoon, as the sun comes out on the bridge and church

The river and fields are awash with flooding in early
December at Radcot

longer, the path will give better access to the countryside for millions of people living in the Thames Valley, especially those without a car.

Originally it had been intended to end the route at Westminster, but with the encouragement of local authorities to the east it was decided to extend the path to the Thames Barrier. It will be a walk through history, for it will take the explorer past such well known landmarks as the Houses of Parliament, Hampton Court, Runnymede, Windsor Castle, Cliveden and Kew Gardens. Its accessibility to town dwellers, passing through such places as Maidenhead, Reading and Oxford, will make it unique.

Starting at the Thames Barrier, the path will go all the way to Ewen, following the original towpath where possible. This has created certain problems, because upstream from Lechlade there never was a tow-path, and for some reason a tow-path was never added to the definitive map as a public right of way in other areas. To overcome this the Countryside Commission has called for new rights of way either along or slightly away from the river bank, using existing paths which divert the route from the bank, or building new bridges. New bridges are also planned at Shepperton, Bourne End, Shifford and Temple.

The proposed route in London runs on both sides of the river, along the riverside only where it is expected that implementation of the route will occur within the next twenty years. In the long term only minor diversions from the riverside will be necessary, but in the meantime some use of roads will be inevitable.

use, it is planned to erect around 1,000 waymarks and 123 information boards and to publish leaflets and guides. The waymarking will enable the entire route to be covered without either guide or map.

The Countryside Commission, which initiated the path, has planned the route to take the best line in terms of the character of the path and the quality of the landscape it passes through. It will thread through Surrey, Berkshire, Oxfordshire, Wiltshire and Gloucestershire. Intended to be just as popular with those seeking a short walk as with those more energetic and out for a weekend or

The start at the Thames Barrier offers one of the best locations to view the river becoming part of the sea. The route will then pass the outskirts and heart of the city, making it accessible to many people living, working in or visiting London.

The introduction of the Thames Path will open up the pleasures of the route to many thousands of people as it runs just inches from the water for many miles. Walkers will not find an easier trail to follow anywhere else in Britain.

On some stretches you will encounter miles of total isolation and therefore capture the true beauty of the river; on others you will find yourself striding through busy towns where the Thames is taken for granted. You will discover that the scenery changes with each passing mile and meet those who have spent their lives within yards of its banks and have no wish to venture further afield. And gradually, as you go forth on your voyage of discovery, you will discover why they feel the way they do.

Late afternoon on a cold January day in Clifton Hampden, looking down on the fine bridge, as the frost settles

WALLINGFORD
The sun comes out on a cold January afternoon

EYNSHAM
After a very cold night in late February, the sun comes out to warm the start of the day; soon it will be March and then Spring once more

INDEX OF PLACES

References to photographs are in italic.

ACKNOWLEDGEMENTS

The authors and publishers would like to thank the following for their cooperation:

Humphrey Carpenter for the use of maps; National Rivers Authority; The Port of Tilbury; Countryside Commission; The River Thames Society; Fuji Film for use of their Airship; Mr Fred Turk, Queen's Swanmaster; Eton College Boat Yard; and Victor who made the Camera.

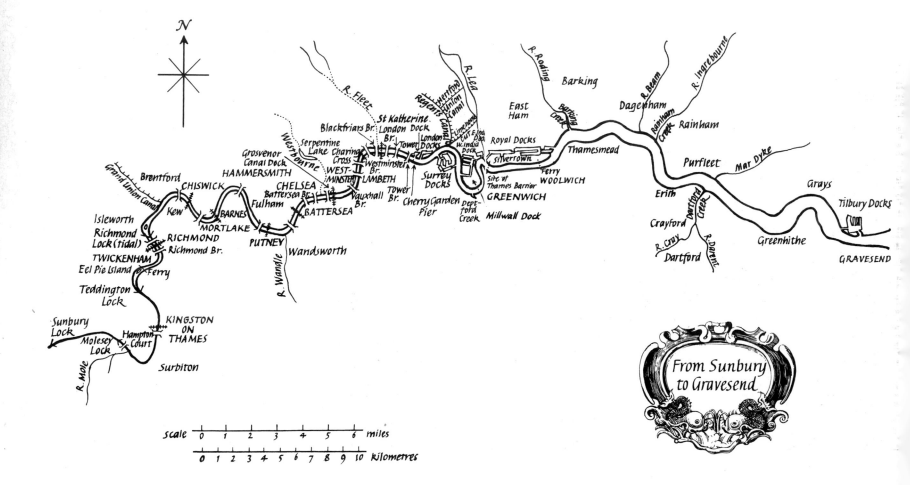

N

R. Fleet

R. Lea

R. Roding

Barking

R. Beam

R. Ingrebourne

Hertford Union Canal

Regent's Canal

St Katherine
London Dock
Blackfriars Br.

Dagenham

Rainham Creek

Rainham

Serpentine
Lake

Grosvenor
Canal Dock

Westbourne

Charing
Cross

Westminster
Br.

Tower
Br.

London Dock

East
Ham

Limehouse

E. India Dock

W. India Dock

Royal Docks

Silvertown

Thamesmead

Purfleet

Mar Dyke

Grand Union Canal

Brentford

HAMMERSMITH

CHISWICK

Kew

BARNES

MORTLAKE

CHELSEA

Battersea Br.

Fulham

WEST-
MINSTER

LAMBETH

Vauxhall
Br.

Surrey
Docks

Cherry Garden
Pier

Deptford
Creek

Site of
Thames Barrier

Ferry

WOOLWICH

GREENWICH

Millwall Dock

Grays

Tilbury Docks

Isleworth

Richmond
Lock (tidal)

RICHMOND

Richmond Br.

BATTERSEA

PUTNEY

R. Wandle

Wandsworth

Erith

Dartford Creek

Crayford

R. Cray

R. Darent

Greenhithe

GRAVESEND

TWICKENHAM

Eel Pie Island

Ferry

Teddington
Lock

Sunbury
Lock

Molesey
Lock

Hampton
Court

KINGSTON
ON
THAMES

Dartford

R. Mole

Surbiton

From Sunbury
to Gravesend

scale 0 1 2 3 4 5 6 miles

0 1 2 3 4 5 6 7 8 9 10 kilometres